The Rantings Of A

Contents

The Nice Bit

This book is dedicated to Barbara and Vincent Wade

Thats my mum and dad, because it is their fault!

My Mum taught me to read before I started school and gave me her love of reading which has stayed with me to this day.

My Dad made me an argumentative bugger and showed me a practical way of working.

They both taught me a work ethic which I hope I've passed on to my kids.

They are also much nicer than me so don't blame

them for the nastier parts
of this book.

Introduction

Firstly let me say this, this book is just my opinion, you may not agree, you may think I'm an idiot, you may be right.

I have no special education; in fact I left school at 15 years old with 4 O levels and have had no formal education since.

However I have spent the 30 years since working all over the world with a massively diverse bunch of people in lots of different countries. I have worked for other people and have owned a successful business and have employed others, I think this gives me a reasonable insight into the world from a few different perspectives, or once again I might just be an idiot.

This book is not about me, it is about you and everyone else in the world, however to understand my perspective it might help to know a brief synopsis of my life. I am going to try to be as truthful as possible but I might miss bits out as my mum might read this one day.

I was born on the 23rd of August 1968 in a small ex mill/mining town in Lancashire called Leigh. My father was a factory worker for BICC which at the time was a massive company making cables for everything from oil rigs to cameras to kettles. My mother was a shop assistant for Woolworths, neither one of those companies exists anymore in the UK which in itself tells a story. I have one sibling, an older brother who as far as I can tell has always had a job but never done any actual work, yep he's an IT guy.

Like so many of my generation I left school with no idea of what I would do and in Thatcher's Britain not too many prospects. Then I was contacted by a company called Ken Wild Management who at the time were the management company for Bucks Fizz who you may remember won the Eurovision song contest in the early 80's.

This management company was running a Youth Training Scheme on behalf of the government to get people working in the entertainment industry. How exciting I thought, I will be working with the Rolling Stones within a few weeks, then they offered me a position in a music shop selling keyboards, against my parents advice I accepted it, acting against my parents advice has become a bit of a theme in my life.

I probably should have listened, but it did lead to other things.

I absolutely hated it. Why would a music shop owner employ a 16 year old, spotty, gobby and totally unmusical lad was a mystery to me, except I was free to him as the government paid my £26.25 weekly wage for him, although I did work Saturdays for which he paid me a princely £6 extra.

It was the hour long bus ride followed by a 15 minute walk to get into Manchester that I hated the most, they don't call it rainy city for nothing.

I asked for a different placement within a couple of months.

They then got me a place at Manchester Apollo, at last I thought, I was then informed it was to work on general maintenance which basically meant fixing seats, this was the last days of the punk era so a lot of seats got smashed every night.

This time I lasted 6 months before asking to move as I at least got to watch a lot of bands for free.

By now I knew what I wanted to do; I quite often saw that a lot of shows had a lighting company from Bolton working for them. I rang up my YTS contact and said I wanted to work for them. She said I couldn't just pick a specific company, I said I could and was doing, after a lot of calls they arranged an interview for me there.

I got the position, mainly because I knew the guys interviewing me from the Apollo I think. When my first year as an YTS was over I was given a pay rise, I was now on £27.50 a week. This doesn't seem like much but a pint of beer was about 50 pence if I had been old enough to drink. I enjoyed working there and learned a lot. Mainly to shut up and admit when I made mistakes, which is possibly the most important lesson I've ever learnt. After a year I was offered a full time job there and £50 a week. I accepted and stayed another 4 years. In that time I went to almost every country in Europe working with lots of different bands such as Shaking Stevens, James Last orchestra, Deacon Blue and lots of others. For a working class lad from Leigh it was a massive eye opener, I saw some things that changed my views on everything from Race to sexuality to politics.

After those years I decided to go self employed, this was against my parent's advice.

I worked for various companies for the next 9 years working for bands such as The Pixies, The Wedding Present, and Gary Glitter (yes him) and also working on conferences for companies like Doc Marten, BT and a host of others. I'd like it on record that the conference industry is possibly the most boring, soul destroying industry in the world. I once spent 4 days, 12 hours a day listening to people talk about fertiliser, and managing to sound like they cared. It's no wonder we all drink too much!

I think it was the conference industry that first made me think about setting my own company up, just so I wouldn't have to do them anymore. At this time I decided I wanted to be a lighting designer, I had been working with lots of designers for a number of years and knew (or thought I knew) a bit about lighting. I became the lighting designer for a few bands such as Teenage fan club, The Icicle Works, Apollo 440 and The Lightning Seeds. But even though I did ok it wasn't really my natural job, I'm not really the artistic type.

At this point I was asked to be the tour rigger on a job, this was a job I had done sporadically over the years so I said yes. This was a bit of a turning point as I've only done rigging ever since, I found my ideal job, very little technology, lots of shouting at people and playing around at heights away from all the real work.

After a short while of using other peoples sub standard equipment I decided to set up my own company.

I did this against my parent's advice.

As of when I'm writing this, in a dressing room at rehearsals for a pop tour, I have had the company for about 15 years, I almost exclusively work for pop acts so have been involved with Boyzone, Westlife, Girls aloud, JLS, Mcfly, The Saturdays to name but a few. In that time I've been to all of Europe, The USA, Canada, Mexico, China, Taiwan, Japan, Australia, New Zealand and lots more that I can't remember. I spent about 8 months touring with One Direction and saw some crazy stuff and met some great people, some lazy useless tossers, a lot of fake people and hangers on and some people that I will be friends with for life. I always get asked the same 3 questions:-

Do I get to meet them?-Yes

What are they like? - 99% are normal polite nice people 1% are not

Can you get me a job? - NO

I think that's enough about me (but if any film producers want the full story it could be arranged for a massive fee)

So I shall move on to what this book is actually about. It is my opinion, if I offend anyone I won't be surprised, if I anger anyone I also won't be surprised, but I think I speak for a lot of hard working decent people who are sick of the way the world is heading,

Then again I could just be an idiot.

I decided to write this as a hobby when touring to try to keep me from being bored, you may be surprised to learn that touring with bands is either really hard work or excruciatingly boring, it's not all drugs and hookers, if fact it's very little drugs and no hookers.

This book will be written over quite a long period of time so when I say an event has just happened it may seem like I'm all over the place time wise, but it isn't written in order and I could be anywhere.

I am writing this book against my parent's advice.

If anyone ever reads this book then I hope you enjoy it, but mainly I just hope that you have paid for it.

Mark Wade.

Religion

What the hell is wrong with people?

How can anyone believe in a god of love and tolerance and yet use that same belief to propagate violence, oppression and intolerance of anyone who doesn't agree with you, even people of the same religion but of a slightly different branch? It is beyond belief that anyone with even a modicum of sense could do this and yet Christians have been doing exactly this for about 2000 years.

Even within just one of the main religions there are a multitude of sects arguing how to pray to the same god

We have the Catholic Church, Orthodox Church, Lutherans, Anglicans, Baptists and Methodists. We have fundamentalist Christianity, Pietism, Evangelicalism, Pentecostalism, Calvinism, Apostolic, African initiated, Jehovah witnesses, Mormons. We have Southcotties, Millerites, Esoteric Christianity, I could go on for pages, even within a sect there are sub sects, just within the Catholic Church we have 22, 23 or as many as 45 (no one seems to know) sub churches such as the Jesuits, the Coptics, the Byzantines, The Ambrosian etc.

Now as we all know Christianity was founded after one group of Jews killed another Jew for saying we should all be nice to each other. The group of Jews responsible blamed the Romans who then spent a few hundred years killing anyone who said the murdered Jew was correct and also happened to be the son of god. After a while the Romans decided that the ones they were killing were in fact correct and took over the full religion and moved its headquarters to Rome. The Romans then decided that anyone who prayed to any other god was wrong and should be killed; also anyone who prayed to the correct god but in the wrong manner should also be killed. Also anyone who argued that you should be allowed to pray to anyone you like in whatever manner you like should also be killed, all the while whilst preaching good will to all men and peace on earth.

As well as Christianity we have a few more large religions, they all seem to suffer from the same problems:-

Within Islam most people have heard of Sunni and Shia who separated in 652AD, however there are also the Kharijite and the Quaranists. The Sunni are separated into about 8 sections and the Shia into about 4.

They don't all get on!

The Hindus have a few sects but seem to quite like each other but are not so keen on the Sikhs. Neither of them are too friendly with the Muslims and no one seems to like the Jews.

Roughly a third of the world is Christian, about a fifth is Muslim, and about a tenth is Hindu and about a twentieth Buddhist and Pagan.

In total about 14% of people are not members of any religious group; I read quite a lot of history and I have never heard of an atheist group starting a war or oppressing people for believing in something that they don't. Don't get me wrong, plenty of wars are started for non religious reasons but are quite often couched in religious terms in order to garner support.

As Hitler showed having a scapegoat is a great way of uniting disparate groups in to a whole. At the moment it seems the Muslims are the Western power's way of gathering support for war which is mainly about oil. No one has suggested invading any country which doesn't have any oil. However the moderate Muslims don't really do themselves any favours when they condemn violence but turn a blind eye rather than actively policing their own back yard. Extremist Imams could be shut down by the massive moderate majority and there would be a lot less violence and much less anti Muslim feeling.

As an atheist I am bemused by the idea of a supreme being, I don't understand how intelligent people can still believe in a God. Back in ancient times when we thought the world was flat, that the sun rose out of the sea and the moon did the same I can understand the need to explain it with a grand Mythical being.

But we now know the earth is a planet, we know the earth orbits the sun. We know the moon orbits the earth. We can split the atom. We have been to the moon. We have produced babies in test tubes and have cloned sheep and pigs. We have flown around the world at the speed of sound and sent a probe to Mars and beyond. We have invented computers with the power of unbelievable proportions, we have discovered antibiotics and we know how gravity works and how the moon affects the tides. And we have worked out the big bang theory. We are close to creating artificial intelligence and household robots are no longer a product of science fiction.

 And evolution! Yes evolution! We know that we descend from apes and that we are genetically related to plankton. We know that there were different types of humans leading up to modern Homo sapiens. We also know that there have been thousands of species of animals, plants and even human types that didn't make it this far, surely a God wouldn't need to practice? And yet the Creation myth is still taught in hundreds of schools, it's like teaching that the heart controls the body rather than the brain, we worked that out about 600 years ago so we stopped teaching it. All the rules of teaching seem to be changed when religion is involved. In no other subject at school are lies, half truths and fabrications taught as truth (except history if you are in North Korea) If you look at science books from the fifties you will find things that are not true, the difference is when scientists discovered that something wasn't true they stopped teaching it.

Three of the biggest religions all started in the same place; they share a lot of the same prophets and all basically believe in the same god. The Jews seem to have started it and have pretty much been consistent in their beliefs. From Judaism came a couple of sects who became religions in their own right, Islam and Christianity, who as we have seen have split into hundreds of different sub sects who don't really like each other.

Now I am a Bolton fan (sad I know) and I have a friend called Bobby who is also a Bolton fan, sometimes I go to matches and sometimes he goes to matches, I like to sit near the front so I can see individual skill but he likes to sit high up to see the overall game better, we both follow the same team but watch in different ways,

So I'm going to kill him, seems fair.

The only real difference is that, I know for a fact that Bolton exists.

We in Britain, in theory, live in a secular society, but do we?

Religion seems to creep into every area of our lives, if you are in court you will be asked to swear on the bible that you will tell the truth, the head of state is also the head of the church of England, which must be a conflict of interest as most people are not members of the Church but she is still their monarch. Bishops sit in the House of Lords and get to vote on laws which apply to us all whether we believe in God or not. Births, Marriages and deaths are officiated by the clergy even if the people in question have never been to church, that of course is hypocrisy on our part and I am as guilty as anyone.

Churches, Mosques and Temples are all registered charities, this means they have massive tax advantages over other businesses, and yes they are a business. A Charity is defined as a nonprofit organization formed to do charitable work; I assume charitable work means doing good deeds for others? I don't see how preaching what I believe to be fanciful fabrications at best or cynical lies at worst can be deemed charitable works.

Incidentally the Church of England is one of the largest land owners in Britain, I wonder how a charity managed to accrue such wealth?

I know that to some people faith is an integral part of their life, I actually wish I did believe as I've often wondered what happens after death. Unfortunately you can't make yourself believe something just because it would be nice. People point out to me that without religion we would have no moral code, that is just silly;

Being an atheist does not make me go out stealing or committing burglary. It doesn't make me have less regard for human life, if anything I have more as I believe this is all we get. It does not make me more likely to commit assault and rape. It does not make me more likely to fiddle my taxes or drive too fast. Being brought up by decent parents achieved all that.

Incidentally the massive cover up by the Catholic church of Priests abusing children should be enough reason for anyone to reject organised religion. Organised religions are not about God, they are about power, influence, wealth and power. The treasures owned by the catholic church could pay enough to sort a serious amount of world problems, but you don't see them selling stuff off on EBAY do you? Every church is permanently begging for money, shouldn't the collection plate go to the areas poor people? I would like to point out that there are some great individual Priests,Vicars, Deacons, Imams and Rabbis who actually care and do a great job. But do we really need them?

And now my question is why?

Why do you personally have to be the one who knows how God wants to be prayed to?

Why do you think God cares as long as we don't commit major sins?

Why would God allow us so many different religions if he does care?

Why, (if everything is God's will), would you try to change what He has decided should be?

And perhaps more importantly than any of that,

Why do you care if I am doing it all wrong?

Surely it means I will go to hell and never bother you again?

But the real problem isn't religion

The real problem is people using religion as a way of justifying their own bigoted and racist views.

People seem to have a problem with anyone that is different to them, I even find myself doing it, if I am working with a group of people from all over the world, I find myself talking to the Europeans more than the non Europeans, The British more than the Europeans, The English more than the British, the northerners more than the southerners and the Lancastrians more than the Yorkshire folk. It's madness!

Of course no one talks to the French.

Prisons

I read the papers quite often; I watch the news everyday when I am in the UK. I like a lot of people am either , disgusted, bemused or downright angry by the stories that the news people choose to cover, and like many others am disgusted, bemused and downright angry at the sentences passed on the people convicted of various crimes and offences.

Now I know the entire liberal PC brigade will hate me for this but Prisons are too easy!

Now I once spent a night in a cell in France (drunken disorderly) and it was a concrete shelf with no heating in a concrete room with a small tin cup full of water and a hole in the floor for a toilet. It was horrible and I had no desire to spend a minute longer in there that I had to, however I was very drunk, totally guilty of being a pillock and deserved every second of it. I also was late for work on a tour with the band 'Suede' and but for my friends covering my back I would probably have been sacked. And I would have deserved that too!

And that is what this chapter is about, if you do something wrong you should accept the punishment if you are caught and convicted. And if you are sentenced to 5 years in prison you should not walk free after 2 years because you didn't kill/rape/steal or attack someone in that sealed environment.

Being well behaved in prison does not make your previous crime any less of a crime for the victim. If you are sentenced to 5 years you should serve a minimum of 5 years, yes a minimum, you should have time added on for bad behaviour.

In the 5 years you are serving you should have very few so called human rights, if a judge and jury decide you are a guilty criminal then you are by definition outside of normal society and all its rules and customs, you can't decide to break some of the rules but then use other ones to make yourself more comfortable.

There has recently been some debate about prisoner's right to vote, what a ridiculous argument. How can anyone say that a convicted murderer or rapist has the same rights as a law abiding person? If you are in prison it's because you broke societies rules, therefore you cannot have a say on how society progresses. Now we all know that prison doesn't work, the liberals would have us believe it is because people just need to be understood and sending them on holiday to Spain is better than locking them up, as prisons are today I would agree.

Prisons should be single stone cells.

There should be minimal heating (it costs tax payers money)

There should be minimal food (it cost tax payers money)

There should be no televisions (it is supposed to be punishment)

There should be no Computer games (it is supposed to be punishment)

There should be no interactions between prisoners (we don't need criminals teaching each other better techniques)

There should be no lighting except when the guards need it (daylight in the day is enough)

Every prison should be the same, no different categories for different crimes.

There should be no rights of visitation (it costs tax payers money)

There should be much better screening to stop drugs and alcohol getting in (no visitors should help with that)

Prisoners should be allowed books to read (it might educate them a little)

Now I know some people are going to say that a murderer and a shop lifter shouldn't have the same punishment, and they are correct. A shoplifter should have only 1 night in my version of a prison and a murderer should never walk free again. I also know that a full life term is deemed cruel and unfair for a murderer but that is exactly what the victim's family receive. Why should a child's mother still be grieving their loss whilst the murderer gets out after 5 years to continue their life?

So if prisons were run as I have outlined then they would cost a fraction of the current cost, prison sentences for minor crimes could be much lighter as everyone would serve the full amount, we would no longer need a parole board as there would be no to parole for them to talk about, saving the tax payer even more money, re-offending rates would fall and no one would commit crime whilst out on parole as there would be none.

Can anyone tell me how an open prison is actually a prison? According to the dictionary a prison is a place where inmates are forcibly confined and denied a variety of freedoms under the authority of the state. How can a place where a person can walk out whenever he or she feels like it be called a prison? It's a joke, but not a funny one. Apparently they have to be in by a certain time of night and can't leave until a certain time in the morning; I've been in guest houses in Blackpool with stricter rules.

I have recently been reading about how many people have walked out of open prisons and never returned, some of these people were arrested for such offences as assault, rape and armed robbery! Unbelievable that any of those types of criminal are in an open prison in the first place, but that they can just walk out is beyond belief. One open prison has up to 95 people missing from it, some of them convicted violent prisons and the local population were not even informed, in fact it only came to light after one of them committed another crime whilst being hunted!

All of the open prisons should be sold off or used for a better purpose such as much needed care for disabled, mental health clinics and elderly care. Once again this would be a saving for the tax payer. Now some people will say that it shouldn't be about saving money for the tax payer, it should be about rehabilitation of offenders.

Now I could be wrong on this but:-

Option 1

Sentenced to 5 years for some crime or other, spend the first year in a closed prison, in this time have access to a television, a play station, 3 square meals a day, daily access to a gym so I can be a stronger thug, days spent talking to other criminals learning how to pick locks, better ways of avoiding detection and gaining underworld contacts for future use. After 1 year I am transferred to an open prison where I am allowed to go out to visit my family with no supervision so I can commit the odd burglary or other crime before going back to my cell for a free meal and some footie on the TV. 6 months later I am released fully fit and trained ready to be a much more efficient criminal. Oh and whilst I am in 'prison' I can vote in whichever party is weakest on enforcing the law, I'd vote Green but they will never get in so Labour it is.

Option 2

I am sentenced to 5 years for some crime or other. I am taken to a cold damp concrete cell where I am fed porridge for breakfast and bread and water for lunch and dinner. I stay in this cell for 5 years. If I commit any transgression of the rules my sentence in lengthened, by 6 months each time seems fair. I am released after 5 years praying I never have to go there again.

Now I'm not a psychologist or a behavioural scientist but I know which one would encourage me to re offend and which one would make me never break the law again.

Now apparently we can't do this as it would be against the prisoner's human rights. I DON'T CARE!

When you steal, mug, rape, murder, molest, attack or even just vandalise you give up your right to be treated the same as the normal, taxpaying, hard working citizens. How can a person who breaks the rules then be protected by them, it does not make sense. Everyone knows that you are allowed to hit back in self defence, surely that must apply to the state too? Once you have been released back into society then yes you should be treated the same as everyone else, but if you are in prison you have put yourself outside of society and should be treated as such.

Of course there will be some re offending, some people are just scum and always will be, anyone who is sent to prison 3 times should be forcibly and irreversibly sterilised, because scum always seem to bring up more scum, and always seem to have more children than normal people, maybe that's why crime figures rise all the time, they are out breeding us! Of course they might not have so many children if they actually had to work to support them, but that is a topic for a different chapter.

And what about crimes where even my version of a prison is too easy?

I am sure that I am not the only person who gets angry and disillusioned when yet another child is attacked, molested or murdered by a person who has committed similar crimes before but is back on the streets after serving a small sentence in our joke of a prison service. It beggars belief that our justice system lets these people out to reoffend. If a person is a proven danger to children then they should never ever be allowed to walk the streets until it is 100% proven they are no longer a risk, how can a perverts rights be more important than those of our children? If we must release them then they should be chemically castrated (or physically) and ankle tagged with all places where schoolchildren are likely to be deemed out of bounds, any transgression, however small should result in them being re imprisoned immediately.

Any person found guilty of murdering a child should be executed.

The state should not protect these people and we should not provide therapy or counselling for them. When the state has been complicit in releasing these people into our society then the people responsible should also be brought to trial and charged with aiding and abetting a paedophile.

Another thing that needs to change is the law on defending your own house, if someone breaks into your property then there should be no limit on how you defend yourself.

It is impossible to accidentally break into my house, even if the front door is wide open I'm sure you are aware it isn't your house, so if i kill, maim or cripple you then it is YOUR fault and it shouldn't even get you a reduced sentence.

One more thing, whatever it does actually cost to imprison someone should be payable by the prisoner, if this means selling their assets when they are in prison or giving them a bill on release then so be it. Why should you and I pay for it? And if they receive a bill then they should be made to pay it off at a reasonable rate, not 5 pence a week as the courts allow with fines, which should also stop.

One more thing (again) The justice system in this country is totally weighted towards the human rights of the criminals and not towards the victims, this is unfair and totally wrong. As far as I can see it then the criminal loses all but their most basic rights until they have faced their punishment. The victim must come first. if a burglar is crippled, disfigured or even killed by the home owner then there should be no consequences for the home owner.

Also (I know) When a man in this country is accused of rape his alleged victim has the right of anonymity, this is of course correct. But the alleged rapist should have the same rights. Far too many times innocent men have been dragged through the papers and sometimes convicted by them before being found not guilty. When this happens the person who made false accusations should be imprisoned for the same length of time as the accused would have faced. Lots of lives and reputations have been ruined by malicious and frankly gold digging women in this country and the accusers seem to get a slap on the wrist if anything. If a man is found guilty of rape then he should obviously go to prison for a long time. Repeat rapists should be chemically castrated though I would have no problem with actual castration, with a rusty knife, in salt water, by a blind man.

Health and Safety

The Health and Safety Executive (HSE) inadvertently cause millions if not billions of pounds to our economy. They make working peoples lives a nightmare, they make jobs more difficult and sometimes make jobs more dangerous.

They rarely make anything safer.

I work in quite a dangerous industry, we routinely hang hundreds of tons of equipment above peoples heads. We use high voltage and high amperage equipment. We build temporary structures at high speed and usually after far too little sleep. We fill trucks (by hand) with tons of heavy, awkward, sharp equipment. We do all this with poorly trained, poorly paid and poorly treated crew. Because of all this you would assume I would want stricter rules on safety and health. And I DO, but only if they actually make it safer rather than tick boxes and cover peoples arses. I have no interest in some bloke who has been on a course which tells him how to be safe on a building site, I'm not a builder.

I have no interest in a bloke who has read a book about being safe but has never ever done the job. I genuinely want to work in a safe environment where there are no injuries or deaths. I want everyone to get enough sleep, be correctly trained and be paid enough that they don't need to work constantly to make ends meet. I work in different venues all over the world but for this i'm going to concentrate on the UK

I can honestly say that there are no 2 venues in all of the UK with exactly the same rules when it comes to safety. Some rules may be the same but the interpretation is vastly different, and every single venue is 100% convinced that they are doing it correctly.

A large part of the problem is that companies make vast profits from supplying "safety" equipment.

High visibility jackets

steel toecap shoes

harnesses

safety signs

flashing beacons

wet floor signs

trip hazard signs

hazard tape

sirens

hard hats

cable ramps

reflective tape

safety glasses

goggles

anti slip tape

hand sanitisers

breathing masks

ear defenders

I could go on but you get the idea.

I think you would agree that most of them are a good idea, but are they?

The hardest colour to see is black (not really a colour I know) but if you put a black ball in a box of white balls then it is the easiest to see, and that is the case with High Vis Jackets, I once was shouted at by a man who ran (which is dangerous at work) to tell me that he had spotted me from about 100meters away as I was the only one not wearing a High Vis Jacket. When I pointed out that I was, by his own words, the most visible, he shouted that rules had to be followed. And there lies the problem, rules that don't make it safer. Anyone who walks down a high street will see an Ocean of high visibility wear, if just one person was wearing one then they would indeed be easier to spot, but as it is the person in black is the most obvious. taking this to a logical conclusion we should all wear different colours. (like we used to)

I recently saw a sign which said "The coffee from this machine may be hot"

If I bought a coffee from a machine and it wasn't hot i'd be pretty bloody annoyed, as would you, so why tell us?

It isn't because we don't know it's hot, it isn't because it will stop us scalding ourselves if we knock it over, and it definitely isn't because the coffee company cares about us, It is because it stops us suing them. So nothing to do with safety at all.

The Health and Safety Executive were set up to provide protection in factories and other work places to stop bosses putting profit before people, no one is going to object to that. Back in "the day" people were killed, maimed and exploited to a shocking degree. So I am not trying to argue that they are a necessary evil. But there is a massive lack of common sense.

If I was to invent a piece ridiculous safety equipment such as a seat belt for Police Motorcyclists then the actual motorcyclists would think it was a waste of time and they would be correct.

But if I did a national campaign to stress the importance of motorcycle seat belts and to stress that the riders were being put at risk by not having them?

I'd probably sell thousands, OK i'm being silly but it is fear of litigation that drives the industry rather than safety.

I know a place where the rules say we need to wear HVJ, even though we are indoors with ample lighting and have no heavy machinery moving around. This same venue allows smoking in an area next to the door, there is a sign at this location which forbids smoking and says you have to wear a HVJ, so the no smoking rule (and LAW) is ignored whilst the HVJ rule in enforced, ridiculous!

There are lots of rules that seem to make sense until they are actually applied, as I have mentioned, one of them is the high vis rule. You are no longer allowed to use a ladder as you might fall off. By this rationale you shouldn't be allowed to cross the road as you might get run over, you shouldn't go upstairs as you might fall down, you should no longer eat food as you might choke and you shouldn't drink water as you might drown.

If you go into any major town or city you will see pedestrians "protected" from the traffic with steel barriers, I can understand it outside a school or play area where children might run out but on every corner? Imaging being a cyclist on the corner when a bus or truck gets too close, previously you would have jumped the kerb or even fell on to it, now you are squeezed through the fence like cheese through a massive grater.

A few years ago there was a case where police and firemen watched a child drown because it would have been dangerous to try to rescue him. This was in 3 Ft of water but even though the individual officers wanted to rescue him they were ordered not to. Personally I would have ignored the orders and I will never understand why they didn't. Apparently anything deeper than ankle depth is deemed too risky.

I have just seen a sign on a truck which said "this vehicle may turn left" I would say that the only people who don't already know this probably can't read anyway. Which nicely brings us to pointless signs. If you buy a bag of nuts it will say on it "may contain nuts" who would have known otherwise? It is reasonable to put that on a ready meal I suppose but on a bag of nuts? We get signs telling us obvious stuff all the time, Signs telling us that there may be ice! Who doesn't know that when it's really cold water freezes? I am not the most observant person in the world but if the signs we see are actually needed then I must be a detective better than the love child of Sherlock Holmes and Miss Marple.

But, for you poorly educated:-

Petrol is highly flammable

Wet floors are slippery

Pebble beaches are uneven

Coffee is hot

There is sometimes a gap

The edge of the cliff is, erm, at the edge

Nuts are made of nuts

When it rains the road will be wet

Hot water can be hot

This is a Step / wall / fence / puddle

Knives are sharp

Falling off a cliff could sting a bit

You shouldn't drink bleach

Dogs sometimes bite

Heavy loads are not light

Forklifts can crush you

Now that I have taught you some useful information to keep you alive I will move on.

If you buy a first aid kit it will no longer have plasters in it, because a tiny, tiny amount of people are allergic to the sticky part and it can make them itch a bit. So we will have thousands of children with cut knees and fingers who are no longer allowed to be tended to.

Bumper cars are no longer allowed to bump as it might cause whiplash. Students have been throwing their mortar boards in the air for hundreds of years, not anymore. They might injure someone.

Postmen have been told to not walk on cobbles if they are wet.

A school in Bristol has banned a blind girl from using her white stick in case it trips someone.

British soldiers can no longer fire live mortars in training as it's a bit loud.

A primary school banned drinks for teachers in the playground in case a child was allergic to any of the ingredients.

Council employees are not allowed to carry anything into your home, even if you are infirm and cannot do it yourself, they might hurt themselves (or have to do some bloody work)

At Christmas time you may want to have some crackers on the table, but if you are under 16 you will need an adult to buy them for you as that massive explosion when they are pulled could take your arm off.

When I was about 12 years old i was shown how to wire a plug, it was very easy and I am pretty sure I have never forgotten how to do it and i've never caused a fire from it, but if I want to wire it now then I need to either get an electrician to do it or to certify it afterwards, obviously I don't but I lie awake in fear that I might be arrested.

It is a legal requirement to have heath and safety notices up in the work place, these show us really useful things, like the correct way to wash your hands, who knew?

They tell us that there are forklifts operating, if you can't see an eight ft high, bright yellow metal monster weighing 3 ton then a sign isn't really going to help is it?

They tell us the floor is wet, just in case that puddle of water was confusing us.

They tell us to wear personal protection equipment even if there are no hazards anywhere.

If the relevant signs are not up then the company can receive hefty fines, when the sign changes the companies have to buy and display the new one, this is very expensive and the H&S do spot checks to fine people but don't publicise the changes, hence it is once again about making money and absolutely nothing about health or safety.

Now this may seem that I hate the Health and Safety Executive, but I don't. They do come out with some very silly rules but for the most part they do a decent job. When we actually look into these rules we usually find that they don't exist or are being used incorrectly.

Most times we run afoul of H&S it is because someone is using it as an excuse to not do their job or not provide a service. When a person says to you "sorry I can't do that because of H&S" they usually mean "I can't be bothered doing that so i'm going to blame the H&S "

And the other times it is a clueless idiot who is trying to justify his own existence by sprouting rules he only vaguely understands. And for the love of god don't give these people uniforms, because they then think it makes them the arbiter of work place justice.

So climb that ladder, throw that ball, wire that plug, skip at school, drink hot coffee, hurdle that fence, work in a black t shirt, take off your hard hat, pet that dog, put a plaster on your child's knee, help that old lady move her television, cross the road, walk near the cliff edge, work without a method statement, take risks, BUT......

Use your common sense.

Most safety equipment doesn't make us safer, hard hats restrict our vision, Hi Vis is a great idea if you are outdoors, at night, near a road, not much point in bright light, indoors, delivering some flowers. Walking on a cliff is perfectly safe unless you are near the edge, if you can't see the edge then you can't see the sign either. If you have allergies then you will check the ingredients, Safety goggles are a great idea when you are using chemicals or cutting wood and metal but they cut down your peripheral vision and are therefore dangerous to walk around with. Soap and water is just as good as sanitisers. Ear defenders are handy when using noisy equipment but can stop you hearing a "watch out mate" when its quiet. Common sense is the real answer to most situations, it may be lacking and in decreasing supply but trying to make the work risk free just makes it worse. If you never need to think then why would you?

So every time someone tries to stop you doing something on the grounds of health and safety, fight them!

I don't mean punch them, though it is always tempting, but fight for common sense, argue with them, be sensible, point out why they are wrong, ask them what training they have to make them understand the risks, ask to see the person who made the rule, ask for it in writing, make their lives as difficult as possible.

Because if you don't it will steadily get worse, you will not be allowed to do anything without a training course that makes it harder and slower and possibly more dangerous.

And it makes life fun, which i'm sure will be banned soon too.

Food, Obesity and Exercise.

Didn't really know what to call this chapter, it's a bit of a mixture of subjects, food and a personal view of what is acceptable, why some people are bloody enormous and why is it cheaper to eat badly than it is to eat healthily?

I'm going to start with a favourite problem I have, mashed potato, I bloody hate it! Why would I want any food pre chewed? I'm not a baby sparrow, i'm not missing all my teeth, I can swallow solids and i'm not going to choke. I can't think of any other food we accept mashed to oblivion as if it is normal. Potatoes can be cooked in so many different ways that surely mashing isn't needed? When i was 6 months old I accepted that my food would be basically a horrible paste, and maybe, just maybe I will need the same in my later years, but I doubt it !

Sorry but I needed to get that off my chest.

Apparently calling somebody fat is now considered a hate crime on the same level as racial or religious abuse, but that's just a myth spread by fatties. If you happen to be fat and you are happy then fair enough, that is up to you, but expecting tax payers to pick up the tab for all the related issues is not ok. Expecting the tax payer to pay for health issues caused by your obesity or benefits because you can't work is just selfish. Some people are going to say that being fat is not their fault, and for a minuscule percentage that is correct, and I will happily pay for all the extra care and attention that you need. But if there were as many people in that condition who claim to be then there would be some evidence. When we see the horrible pictures from Africa of people starving I have never noticed the odd fat one, there is never a couple sitting there claiming they have big bones and a gland problem. So how come it is only in the West where people seem to have this problem?

Because diet coke and a pizza is not going to work, thats why!

It is no coincidence that the majority of large people are in the poorest areas, every poor neighbourhood seems to be overrun with chip shops, indians take aways, pizza places and bakers. If you want some fresh fruit or veg then you need to get to somewhere that sells it, not always easy for the poorest people out there. But not everyone is fat, which means that the thin ones are doing something different, like exercise, eating properly, not drinking beer all the time. It doesn't seem that hard really, But we all know that a good takeaway is just heaven, but we also try not to have them too often.

As you may have gathered I have very little time for people who don't help themselves, people who blame their every problem on others, on society, other parents, on where they were born, on their birth sign or just about anything but themselves.

I once watched a girl sitting on a wall eating a pizza big enough to use as a bin lid and then a couple of cakes, now this was a big girl, the wall was under serious stresses. I happened to follow this girl inside where she went and sat with a group of normal size friends. They were ordering lunch at a well known Mcburger place. I heard the girl in question say, with a straight face I might add "I'll just have some fries and a diet coke, I don't eat much"

I was amazed and a couple of her friends didn't look convinced either, but that is the problem, firstly that she refused to accept that she is massive because she eats so much, secondly because she involves others in her fantasy, and thirdly because her friends don't tell her to stop lying and stop eating enough to feed a pod of whales.

What bemuses me the most is the total lack of self respect.

50 years ago there were very few obese people, there were some but most of those were genuinely not at fault, although there were of course some gluttons. But back then most people could not afford to be fat so it was mainly the preserve of the wealthy. Food is cheap and plentiful, you can eat a meal for a couple of pounds quite easily, Of course that makes over eating far too easy, but that can't be the only reason can it?

When I was about 12 my Friends asked me if I fancied cycling to Manchester airport with them, I didn't even think about it, I just said yes ok, it was about 25 miles as we couldn't use the motorway.

We used to cycle everywhere, If i asked my parents for a lift the answer would invariably be, you've got a bike haven't you?

I did have a bike, it weighed just less that a ton and had 5 gears. It wasn't a bike like we have today, it didn't have 93 gears and weigh less than a small twig, consequently my friends and I were thin, fit and also very happy. We used to meet up and go swimming, we played football (badly in my case), We walked miles to meet friends and never thought anything of it. I know I sound like a grumpy old git but Im not honest! I play computer games, I have a smart phone on which I use Facebook and play games and check E mails, yep in that order. But a smart phone should be there to help your life rather than be your life.

Compare that to some kids today, sitting on the sofa, playing computer games where they pretend to ride a bike whilst being brought sugary snacks and soft drinks by an over indulgent parent.

Watch kids on the bus, on smart phones texting and watching videos.

Watch kids walking down the street, texting and looking at you tube.

Watch kids at pop concerts, texting and videoing, rather than actually watching it and enjoying it.

Watch kids sitting with their friends, texting and sending pictures to each other.

The smart phone is the biggest danger to the health of the country than any other factor.

If you must give your kids a smartphone then at least make them earn it, make them do sport, learn an instrument, learn a language, other than text speak and Americanisms, Make them ride a bike to school once in a while, make them walk short journeys, serve water at meals, make fast food a treat rather than the norm, because once in a while is fine.

The most annoying thing about all the above is that everyone already knows it all, but people are more worried about what little Timmy wants than they are about what is good for him.

When Jamie Oliver tried to make school meals healthy there were cases of Mums sneaking junk food into schools so little Loretta didn't throw a tantrum, It beggars belief. So if you are reading this and you have fat kids then let me be plain;

It IS Your fault!

When Timmy and Loretta are morbidly obese later in life you can console yourself that at least spoiling them was an easier option. You can tell everyone they are big boned or it's their glands or the pixies force fed them at night. Or you can start looking after them properly, you can give them healthy food and deal with the tantrums, you can make them use a bike rather than drive them everywhere, you can make them walk short journeys. And while they are walking and cycling you will have more free time, so you can make real food rather than ready meals and fizzy drinks.

Once again this all boils down to responsibility, nothing is ever anyones fault.

If you trip over a broken flag stone your fist reaction should be, "oops I need to look where I'm going" rather than "how much can I sue the council for"

When a car crashes into the back of you, you should think "I hope no one is hurt" not "ooh whiplash, I'll get a holiday out of this"

And it's the same with fat people, whether it is blaming mythical diseases or suing the burger shop it is never their fault, but anyone who has ever put a bit of weight on and then lost it again will know, yes it bloody well is. There seems to be a massive rise in the number of diabetics, for some it is hereditary and no ones fault, for others it is brought on by consuming too much sugar, and I was warned about that when I was a child so it isn't like nobody knows the cause, but like smokers and heavy drinkers they just carry on and then let us tax payers pick up the bill.

I have been known to drink too much, I used to do it regularly, and if at some point in the future it catches up with me, I will not be suing the breweries, because it will be my own stupid fault!

That is enough about our larger friends.

A while ago there was a fuss in the papers about horse meat being found in burgers, We are a strange race us English when it comes to food. Just because some people like horses it is frowned upon to eat them, a person who will happily eat a steak from a cow every day will be consumed with anger at eating a similarly sized horse. I just think they should have labelled them truthfully, "may contain Shergar"

And dogs, similar size to a sheep, a mammal like sheep and us. Probably a reasonable amount of meat, what is the problem?

Because dogs have personalities and are smart, just like pigs then but a lot of us like a bacon buttie.

Chicken and duck is fine but not swans for some reason, the queen disapproves I suppose?

Some countries eat just about anything and they seem to do ok, apparently they eat guinea pigs in Peru but god forbid we could eat a cat.

But we happily feed horse to dogs which seems quite ironic.

Any market in the north of England and beyond will sell tripe, It is possibly England's worst food item, I would rather eat dog, cat or horse than eat a cow's stomach, but some people love it.

In Scotland they eat haggis, traditionally a sheep's stomach filled with offal and grain, It's lovely if you have never tried it.

I've never attempted to eat a deep fried Mars bar.

We have recently started to experiment a bit more, you can now buy Ostrich, Alligator, Kangaroo and even Buffalo, but Horse is still a step too far.

How do you know when a vegan is in the room? Because they tell you!

My god they annoy me, especially the fake ones;

The ones who loudly announce they are vegan whilst wearing leather shoes and drinking a trendy microbrew beer. Not realising that most beer contains fish. And leather comes from cows.

I don't understand why anyone would discount eating about 80% of their choices just because it comes from an animal. We have sharp teeth for a reason, and it isn't for eating vegetables, Cows don't have sharp teeth for the same reason, they don't rip meat apart. Scientists say we would never have evolved such high intelligence without meat as we need a massive amount of protein to grow brains. So according to science vegetarians are not as intelligent, but we knew that already. I am not a fan of the traditional British Sunday roast,

But it is better than Veg and 2 Veg.

Race relations

Bule, Haole, Charlie, Cracker, Mangia cake, Gringo, Peckerwood, Gubba, Gweilo, Honky, White bread, Ghost, Anglo, Bai Tou, White Devil, Whitey, Trog, Snowman, Saltine, Redneck, Palangi, Milky, Kwai lo and Hay seed are all apparently racist terms for me, I'm a pretty normal white guy from Lancashire and I have personally heard about 5 of these before; I have had 2 at the most directed at me and have been offended by exactly none of them. I was once threatened by a black man for being white whilst waiting for a taxi in Bolton. I didn't put this down to him being black though, I put it down to him being a dickhead, I have been threatened by more whites than blacks and again it wasn't because they were white but just dickheads.

Too many people of all races and creeds are far too quick to play the race card in this country.

If I call you a name you don't like it might not be because I'm white, it might be that I'm in a bad mood and you just happen to be there, in which case I'm a dickhead, but not a racist, even if you are black, or Asian, or Oriental. Or maybe, and wow this is groundbreaking, unbelievable stuff, just maybe you deserved it because YOU were being a dickhead? We all are sometimes.

In this world of political correctness it seems that someone will get offended at just about anything, usually the most offended is a Guardian reading white guy who doesn't like the joke about a black man, even though almost all black men are laughing at it. It seems I can tell a joke about a ginger person (at least at the moment) and that is fine, but if I tell a joke about a black or Asian person then I'm a racist. I am not a racist, I do tell jokes that are racist. I also tell jokes about women; does that mean I hate my mother and my daughter? Of course it doesn't. I have told jokes about Blacks, Asians, Chinese, French, women, dwarves, and tall people and about our friends the Irish, so according to the PC brigade I hate all of those groups; I obviously don't. Being offended seems to be the British national pastime at the moment, which is strange as it is the British ability to laugh at ourselves that is one of our greatest strengths.

When I was about 18 I discovered a new band, they were a rap group from America with the daring name 'Niggers with Attitude' and they were Black, and they were like a breath of fresh air after the likes of Spandau Ballet and Duran Duran. Between NWA and Run DMC I was hooked. Rap music did more to change my attitude about race than a thousand articles in the Daily mirror and speeches at school ever did. Music has always been a bit impervious to racism, how can anyone not appreciate the talents of Stevie wonder and Marvin Gaye?

But how come a Black bunch of rappers can call themselves Niggers, but I can't? I even feel uncomfortable typing it. All white people just call them NWA because we are too scared to say it.

I have a friend from Scotland, we routinely tell jokes about him being mean, ginger, subject to the English, him wearing a skirt, eating porridge and anything else we can think of. Not once has he seemed offended or upset about it, not once has he sulked, cried or rang the police to complain of being racially abused.

I grew up in a small town in Lancashire and I was about 13 before I even saw someone who wasn't white, and I remember that when a

Black family did move in we were naturally curious but as far as I remember we didn't really think anything about it. The older generation was less tolerant but I don't think I can be blamed for that.

I am not for one second saying that there are no racist people or racist views in this country. I know that there are some truly horrible, bigoted and racist people. I know that certain groups of people hear racist and derogatory words on a daily basis. And I also know that is unacceptable, however shouting "Racist" every time someone is rude or mean doesn't help the situation as it makes the real cases less believable.

I was once in a pub where the barman was of Asian descent and he refused to serve my friend for being racist, the reason he decided he was racist was because of a tee shirt he was wearing. Now if this tee shirt had been a KKK or BNP shirt then that would be fair, but it was a tee shirt advertising a beer called "Black

Sheep Ale" from a company called "Black Sheep Brewery" now this was in a large pub in Bournemouth which advertised itself as a real ale pub! Could that be a more ridiculous situation?

Incidentally it's a lovely beer.

Some people are just racist and they always will be, it is mainly due to their parents, partly due to their friends and acquaintances and in some cases due to the people of other races they have met. Not all people are nice, there are horrible, lazy, selfish, people from every race and from every religion, there are also nice, respectful, hard working decent people from every race and religion.

If the very first time you meet a person from another racial group they turn out to be horrible, and if you are not educated or intelligent enough then it could make you think all people from that group are like that.

Obviously it is a stupid viewpoint but we have no shortage of stupid and uneducated people. And even most of them manage to work out that 1 person doesn't represent their whole race.

There are certain places in the UK where white people are a minority or even not there at all. Setting up closed communities of any racial group (including white) is instantly going to be a problem for some people. When an area becomes exclusively all black, all white or all Asian it is going to fuel the fires of racism. This is especially true when an area is seen as being taken over and areas that people grow up in are suddenly a no go area. This can and does happen.

Almost every major city in the western world has a China town, somehow this doesn't seem to cause much anger even among the normally racists amongst us. It could be because all people are encouraged to visit to spend money in the multitude of shops and restaurants. But I think it's because the Chinese have integrated into whichever society they choose to live in.

When I was doing a bit of research I was wondering what religion the Chinese were, I had always assumed they were all Buddhists. I was wrong, almost 50% are non religious, about 30% follow Chinese religions, around 7% are Christians, 2% are Muslims (that's still about 27 million) and only about 8% are Buddhist. But they never seem to mention it, they never ask for the laws to be changed to suit their set of beliefs. They dress the same as the general population; they abide by the same rules and don't ask for special schools to be funded by the state.

In short they integrate.

Just after World War 2 the city of London invited West Indian men to drive buses as there was a shortage of drivers, these men were an invaluable resource to the lifeblood of the city. They naturally brought their wives and children with them who brought with them the foods and culture of the West Indies with them. These people dressed the same as the indigenous population; they didn't ask for special schools and they abided by the same rules as the general population.

In short they integrated.

Now I am aware that both Chinese and Blacks have suffered racial abuse and attacks over the years, I think it is improving, but there are always going to be some racists because there are always going to be stupid people.

I am not for one second saying that anyone coming to live in the U.K. should instantly forget their own culture or stop practicing their own religion, but speaking fluent English should be a requirement, as should obeying the laws of this country not the ones allegedly written by some guy a couple of thousand years ago in a tent somewhere. I have no problem with anybody following the rules of their religion as long as they don't conflict with the laws of the nation that THEY have chosen to live in.

I recently heard that a good way to help with racial harmony was for the British Government to apologise for all the people that were murdered, enslaved, resettled and bullied in the building of the British Empire. Almost ever European country had oversea colonies at some point, we only have to look at the spread of languages all over the world, in parts of Africa there are people speaking English, French, German, Dutch and many more, in South America people speak French, Portuguese, Spanish and English. Everyone was doing the same as the British; we just seemed to be better at it. Whereas I agree that the British did some truly horrible things and were responsible for some totally dreadful deeds, I don't see how an apology can help.

No one alive today was responsible!

If after receiving an apology are all those nations going to issue a thank you for giving them doctors, railways, democracy, sanitation? It is a bit like the Monty Python sketch, "what have the Romans ever done for us? And it is just as ridiculous, how far back in time would they have us go?

Maybe the Pope should apologise for one of his predecessors splitting the Americas between Portugal and Spain, maybe the Belgians should say sorry for their empire where over 10 million people were slaughtered? Maybe the French should get on bended knees to beg forgiveness for fermenting civil war in England for hundreds of years, and maybe Germany should say they regret the Nazis a little bit?

I would also like to point out that Britain was one of the first developed countries to abolish slavery, though I do acknowledge that quite a few of our great cities were built by slaves.

And whilst we are on the subject of slavery, at least half of the slaves shipped to the Americas were white; some historians say it is far more than half. The word 'slave' itself comes from the Slav people who were enslaved so much that their very name came to mean it. White men, women and children have been slaves to a much larger degree than any other racial group and for far longer. Ottoman and Arab raiders used to kidnap white Christian children and bring them up as Muslims to fight for their empires as Janissaries which was a kind of enforced foreign legion. The Romans had slaves of every colour and creed but only black slavery seems to be important, surely all slavery is wrong, no matter what colour a person happens to be?

I would also like to point out that a large number of slave traders in Africa were local black men, usually selling people from rival tribes. When are they going to be asked to say sorry?

Would it really help?

We cannot change history and we definitely should not rewrite it.

TAXES

Income tax, Value added Tax, Fuel tax, Road tax, Capital Gains Tax, Corporate Tax, Dividend Tax, Inheritance Tax, Stamp Duty, Stamp Duty Land Tax, Stamp duty Reserve Tax, Air passenger Duty, Council Tax, Customs Duty, Insurance Tax, Landfill Tax, T.V. Licence, Tobacco Tax, Alcohol Tax, Climate Change Levy, Nation Insurance and Aggregate Levy.

Yep that's a lot of taxes and you pay almost all of them, one way or another the government takes a massive amount of your hard earned wages and spends it how they see fit. The problem with having so many different types of taxation is that it makes it almost impossible to see how much they take from us and also very difficult to tell if another political system would have us pay more or less. Maybe that is the idea.

Now you may think this is an unworkable idea but why can there not be just one tax? Every person and every organisation could pay the same rate of tax but with no exemptions, no loopholes, no offshore accounts, no claiming the profits were generated elsewhere (yes you Starbucks, Facebook and Google)

Controversially I think charities should also be subject to the same tax rates.

The reason for this is that a massive number of charities are not really charities. How are religious groups charities? The Church of England is the largest landowner in England yet it has charitable status, this means it is tax exempt but the people who pray and attend church are not, these are often the poorest and least able members of society. The church and other organisations also benefit from Gift Aid, this means they can claim back taxes that YOU paid to benefit themselves yet again. This is lost revenue to the government, and guess who funds the shortfall?

Charities are specifically about one issue, some people will happily give money to look after blind donkeys and refuse to give money to more worthy (in my opinion) causes such as cancer research or save the children. Whether or not you agree with my choices is irrelevant, what matters is that all charities have their supporters and all have their detractors or at best indifference. So why should they be tax exempt? If you want to give some of your hard earned money to look after blind donkeys or a retirement home for bankrupt bankers or a self help group for retired crack whores then that is totally up to you and I commend your selflessness, but I don't think I should have to help fund it. As soon as any institution is given any type of tax break then I and you the taxpayer are paying more taxes as a result. I really don't care that much about Blind donkeys or crack whores and even less about praying to a man in the sky, no matter which version of him (or her) that it may be. I am totally in favour of religious tolerance and would not want to see anyone persecuted in any way for their beliefs, but I don't see why it should be paid for by us.

Whilst we are on the subject of charities I also don't think working for a charity should pay someone a 6 figure salary, maybe if they were properly taxed that would end too.

Back to the idea that everyone should pay the same rate, at first glance this may seem like a bad idea. Surely rich people should pay a higher rate? Why? If you pay 20% of a million pounds then you will be pay a lot more than someone paying 20% of £20,000. Let's not forget that with all the loopholes and offshore accounts removed they will actually pay more than they do now.

If we also taxed all corporations and companies at the same rate then there would be no avoiding tax by saying it is capital gains rather than just profit, at the end of the day profit is profit, taxing it in different ways only benefits the super rich as they have the means to avoid it. As an added bonus to doing it this way we wouldn't really need accountants anymore, maybe they would get proper jobs which actually contribute something and stop being such boring, miserable bastards?

Another plus point on this is that as all money is now taxed and collected in the UK the money is more likely to be banked in the UK as there would be no advantage of moving it offshore. Money kept in the U.K. generates interest in the U.K. which is also taxed in the U.K. and is also more likely to be spent in the U.K. all of which boosts the U.K. economy.

And then we get to the taxes that just shouldn't exist:-

Inheritance tax is disgraceful!

Every penny I have in the bank is money I have earned and been taxed on, whether it is £5 or 5 million makes no difference.

It should not be taxed again, if I have the brains and the work ethic to make money then I have every right to pass that on to my children.

Inheritance tax is all about jealousy, I was born in a council house and when my parents do eventually die they will no doubt leave myself and my brother a very modest amount (hopefully not for many years). However there are people who inherit hundreds of millions of pounds, not only is this none of my business but it is immoral to tax them because I feel hard done by.

I would love to be given millions of pounds but I refuse to begrudge anyone for their parents hard work. We live in a free country and anyone can become rich if they work hard enough and have enough ambition.

Recently there was talk of a mansion tax, for all the reasons above this is also an immoral tax. There are people living in houses that have been in their families for generations, some of these houses have risen in value and are now worth a lot of money. we should be looking at the reason the house prices have risen so much, it is partly down to successive governments failing to build enough council house to keep up with demand, also partly down to planning rules being too strict, and partly down to uncontrolled immigration. All of these examples are the governments fault, the same people who now want to tax someone who lives in a big house that was previously not worth so much.

Business rates are yet another unfair tax, I personally pay a massive amount of business rates on a warehouse I own, for this money I receive nothing, it doesn't matter if 500 people work in that building or none(as is the case) it doesn't even cover getting the bins emptied, there is another charge for that.

T.V. licence is also an unfair tax, there are hundreds of channels but you have to pay for a few of them just to own a television, even if you don't watch them, I know it isn't a lot of money but having done some work with the BBC I have seen the vast amount of wasted money and overpaid staff. Incidentally the independent companies are almost as wasteful but at least I am not paying for them.

It may seem that I am anti taxes but I am not, it is obvious that the government needs to be funded to pay for all the things that we need them to do. We do need Police, Fire service, Hospitals and Doctors, We have to have Roads and trains and Internet and all the other things that we need to make the country work. We need to equip and pay for armed forces and ships and tanks and missiles.

But as with so many other things the amount of wastage and bad management is astounding.

Council budgets are more about empire building than they are about providing services. it is no surprise that most council work is done near the end of the tax year, this is so they have no money left and can claim they need more next year, it is never about improving roads, schools or hospitals. And the bureaucracy ! its amazing, The father of a friend of mine used to work for the council, he used to drive around and every time he saw a pot hole he would stop and fix it, seems simple doesn't it?

Not these days, He is happily retired but that isn't the reason our streets are full of holes.

When a pot hole forms today it just sits there getting bigger until it is reported, then a team is sent to assess it, they then report back that there is a pot hole and draw a yellow ring around it, then it is added to a massive list of the pot holes where it waits its turn, a pot hole repair crew eventually gets to it and eventually fixes it. this same team has probably driven past or around it on their way to other pot holes hundreds of times but they have to wait to fix it until its turn comes up.

"what does this have to do with taxes?" I hear you ask

This costs a lot of money

So taxes are higher!

Political Correctness

Oh Bugger off !

I'm quite tempted to just leave it at that as it pretty much sums up my feelings about this. But I had better explain.

I have covered this a little in other chapters and I may repeat myself a little, please don't get annoyed about this as I might find your views very offensive and could end up with hurt feelings, and I would need a safe space to occupy whilst I talk about my angst at your thoughtless.

OR, I might just ignore you, because I'm not Mard! (Mard is a northern word meaning really bloods soft, or sensitive if you want to be mard about it)

As you may have gathered I'm not a big fan of the P.C. Brigade.

The P.C. Brigade has ruined this country, people are scared to make jokes, scared to speak their own views, scared to say how they voted, scared to take risks, scared to have fun, scared to let children have fun, scared of showing compassion, scared of using certain words, scared of being sued, scared of upsetting people, scared of doing their jobs properly, scared of being scared.

Just scared really.

And why?

If you tell a joke where the subject of the joke is any ethnic group, any religion, any nationality, any type of disability, short, tall, fat, thin, sexy, ugly or indeed any combination of the above then someone will be offended. Now I appreciate that some jokes are invented purely to denigrate and oppress certain groups and no one wants to see a return to that kind of racist and Xenophobic behaviour. But that does not mean we shouldn't be allowed to laugh at people. I work with a very diverse bunch of people. If we can't find a reason to take the Mickey out of you we will usually just make one up. When I am working there are usually people from all over the world, of many different religions and every colour of skin you can get. No one cares. We tell jokes about each other constantly, whether it is about regional accents, (Brummies / Geordies) certain areas being inbred (yes you Isle Of Mann), People being subject to the English (Scotland / Wales), I could go on for ever, there are very few boundaries and we are usually one big happy family. If we talked the way we do in a modern office then I am sure we would all be fired / sued / suspended or Imprisoned. And that is bloody ridiculous, People have forgotten how to have fun.

The British peoples greatest gift to the world is comedy and it is stifled to the point of death by P.C twaddle.

"I disagree with everything you say, but I will defend to the death your right to say it", The great Libertarian Voltair said that (or something along those lines)

I bet he is spinning in his grave, These days you cannot say anything remotely controversial without being pilloried and abused and even assaulted. People should be allowed to not only have their own opinion but be allowed to speak it, even if it is ridiculous and obviously drivel. Being stupid is not a crime, if I want to believe that a certain colour of skin makes me a better person than someone with a different colour then I should be allowed to say it. Banning certain words and opinions makes them more prevalent rather than less, impressionable idiots will always gravitate to banned things, hence the drug problems.

Who did you vote for?

I personally voted UKIP.

NO, I am not a racist, I am not xenophobic, I do not want to curb immigration and I do not want to deport anyone not from here. My reasons for voting UKIP are mixed and would take a chapter of their own. I may vote for someone else next time, presumably that would be acceptable? Who knows ? But whether I voted Labour, UKIP, BNP, Liberal or even Monster raving loony I should be allowed to say so without being called names and accused of being racist / communist / warmonger or anything else. I have no problem with you disagreeing with me but the P.C. brigade only want free speech when it is their version of it.

FUN ! Does anyone remember that? The P.C. Brigade try to stop lots of fun, they try to ban films for being too violent or too racist or too explicit. Why is it up to other people if I want to want Rambo shoot 5000 people or if I want to watch a skinhead gang fighting with Asians or a man and woman or man or men or both having sex together? It really is no ones business but mine. I and I think most people are clever enough to seperate drama from reality. Just because people leave Bruce Lee films kicking each other and making noises like a meerkat. That doesn't mean we will all start shooting people and fighting in gangs and suddenly becoming sexually liberated and promiscuous. But the P.C. brigade says it does. Around the world millions of people play GTA and Tomb Raider. This hasn't seen a marked increase in car theft, nor has it seen thousands of people going all time team and digging up pyramids and stuff.

Anyone fancy a game of Conkers?

Sorry we can't ! You might lose an eye or break a finger or accidentally hang yourself with the string.

Lets have a sports day instead, but you are not allowed to win, because if you win then someone has to lose. That child could then grow up to think that in life there are no winners, no successful people, no one gets paid more than anyone else and everyone has equal talents. You can give them a medal for taking part but not for being fastest.

"See that kid over there? Thats him the one who has finished whilst you are not ever half way, that's Usain Bolt, I know he has finished but you are equal to him in this event because you entered."|

What a load of crap.

Kids will not all be rich, they won't all be successful, some will be junkies, thieves, rent boys, drug dealers, murderers and even politicians and some actually WILL be fighter pilots , footballers, top models, singers and CEO's

Teaching children that taking part is the same as winning is just setting them up for a massive fall and is partly responsible for our sense of entitlement culture.

By the way, you are entitled to nothing, absolutely nothing.

Recently a friend of mine who is a teacher was reprimanded in school for giving a little boy a hug, the boy who was about 7 years old had fallen over and was crying, the teacher gave him a hug, put a plaster on his knee and comforted him until he stopped crying. Basically treated him with compassion. NOT ALLOWED! Apparently this could have been construed as grooming a child and could have led to possible criminal charges. Really?

The child's parents were informed of the "incident" and thanked the teacher for looking after their son. The incident took place in a full classroom, everybody was dressed and She has never been a BBC presenter or a priest.

Now lets get down to the nitty-gritty, oops sorry we can't, that word is banned as it is so obviously racist, you can't write it on the blackboard, sorry Chalkboard, you would need to erase it from the whiteboard, sorry again, dry wipe board, and even if you did write it some vandal would remove it. Sorry not Vandal, I mean a Hooligan, Damn I mean a destructive man, sorry person.

Hip Hip Hooray! Ah bugger can't say that either! I mean dash it. This is too much, I'm going to go outside and have a picnic. Sorry i'm having a packed lunch in a field.

Confused?

Apparently, Nitty-gritty is a reference to the bottom of a slave ship, blackboard/whiteboard is racist, Vandal refers to a germanic tribe and hooligan means an Irish drunkard, Hip Hip Hooray is what the Nazis shouted when hunting Jews and a Picnic is in reality an

American Lynching party, and Bugger is a term for a Bulgarian Homosexual.

WHO KNEW?

BLOODY NO ONE, thats who!

Which is why it doesn't matter, the original meaning of the words may indeed be racist, homophobic and offensive but that isn't how they are used. Language evolves and lots of words mean totally different things now than they did originally, If we talked about these things in their original context then of course we shouldn't use them, but they are used innocently and should not be another battle field for small minded bigots like the P.C. Brigade.

There are very few words that should be banned, any word can be offensive if it is used in an offensive way, but unless the speaker is purposely being offensive then they should usually be given the benefit of the doubt. Lots of older people use what some would call racist terms to describe people of ethnic backgrounds. This isn't because they are racist but is just the way people used to talk all the time. Where I grew up people would routinely say they were off to the "Paki Shop" there was absolutely no malice meant or taken, but say that now and someone will get upset, probably a white guardian reader.

There seems to be a trend at the moment for renaming buildings as they are named after people who were slave owners. Bristol Colton hall is a great old building which hosts concerts and events and has done for decades. The P.C. people want to rename it, I understand that some people think it is celebrating the man but i personally think it should stand as a reminder of past wrongs. Calling it the Dalai Llama hall won't erase the past evils but will just make people less aware. In Leicester almost everything seems to be named after a man called De Montfort. This man was a great general but also a slave trader. He won lots of decisive battles and contributed greatly to the Empire. When all the buildings were originally named the people of Leicester made a choice, just because we hate what he did it makes no sense to try to erase history.

A few years ago the police uncovered a Paedophile ring, this was being run by predominantly Asian men, out of fear for being branded racist the police did nothing about this for years. Tens or even hundreds of vulnerable young girls were systematically abused, raped, passed around like toys, beaten and threatened with death all because the P.C.Brigade had made the conditions so ridiculous that perceived racism is worse than child rape. I am pretty sure that t every single member of the decent law abiding Asian community would rather be interviewed than one child be abused in this way. The police in question and every person who contributed to that P.C. atmosphere should hang their heads in shame and live with the guilt for the rest of their lives.

So P.C. Brigade

you can bugger off

WOMEN and Equality.

Is it just me or are all women mad?

I have no problem with women, I don't think men are superior to women and I believe that women should have equal rights, equal pay and for this they should do an equal amount of work to an equal standard in an equal amount of time. But that isn't what actually happens is it?

I am stronger than most women, I do a physical job which most women and to be honest a lot of men could not do. If when I am working I find myself having to do my job with a person who cannot do the job properly then that puts me in danger of being injured. I do not want to work with that person and I do not believe that person should be paid the same wage as someone who can actually do the job.

It doesn't matter if the other person is male or female, if they cannot do it they should not be employed. I know some ladies who are strong enough and to be honest they are usually better than most men as they seem to be more conscientious, I also know some ladies who cannot do, but we are not allowed to sack them as that would be deemed sexist, I also know a few men who cannot do the job and I would like to sack them too.

I have a friend who is a fireman; the fire brigade now has a quota of women that they have to employ. My friend tells me that lives are at risk because they have to employ women who would not pass the fitness test that the men have to pass, that is not equality but dangerous political correctness. Why should a test be different for women than it is for men? The job doesn't get easier because a woman turns up to do it!

Political parties also have quotas for the number of women who stand for election, again this can only mean a lessening of standards, not because women are less gifted or capable but because if only one lady wants the job she will automatically get it, even if she is as thick as a gatepost, I know we have had some truly inspirational women in politics but this is not the way to get them.

In my job I work with lots of women, I have employed women and have worked for women, I have never had a problem working with someone because they happened to be female, I have however had a problem working with people who are incompetent at their jobs, some happened to be women and some happened to be men.

I was once working in Nottingham and had a lady working with me, when I asked her to lift something for me she told me it was too heavy and to get a man to do it. When I asked her if the men got paid more than she did I was informed that they all got the same wage, I asked her how that was fair if she wasn't capable of doing the job, apparently this was a sexist viewpoint, I don't agree, same wage but does less work? How is that fair? Incidentally I have had similar words with men who couldn't do it either.

There are some things that women do better than men, some of these things are very important and some are not. Women are better at bringing up children than men are, this is possibly the most important thing that anyone ever does but I know I have just offended a large number of women just by saying it. I also know there are bad mothers and some great fathers, but I am talking in general terms here.

Men have better spacial awareness than women; this makes us better at parking cars and visualising how things could be, not as important as raising children I'm sure you would agree.

Men are stronger and faster than women, we are also more aggressive which can lead to all sorts of problems. We all know that if women were in charge then there would be much less conflict in the world.

But it's all changing,

Women seem to be trying so hard to be perceived as equal that they are getting aggressive, less feminine and at the same time men seem to trying so hard to prove they are sensitive and non threatening that the two sexes are meeting somewhere in the middle, and it is ridiculous!

Men should be men, and women should be women, we are different and we should be, without feminine qualities the human race would have died from neglect and indifference thousands of years ago, without masculine qualities we would have starved to death even earlier. People will point out that we no longer live in caves and hunt our food and that we no longer need those qualities to survive, and they might even be correct.

But I like women to be feminine and soft and fluffy, I like the fact that women have totally different perspectives on a range of issues, I think it would be a boring world if men and women wanted to watch the same sports and the same television programs and read the same books and talk about the same things all the time. I also believe that very few women want a man who wants to sit knitting, wears a onesie, likes pictures of kittens and cries watching Bambi.

I think most women want a man who is strong and masculine and who isn't going to burst in to tears for no apparent reason. Again I could be wrong but I don't think so.

I would also like to point out that I am not anti women or anti women's rights. I know that some women have contributed massively to the human race as a whole. Marie Curie springs to mind, I also know that women invented so many different and useful things, Kevlar was invented by a woman as was the circular saw, the syringe and liquid paper are also there, so are the dishwasher, the rolling pin, the windscreen wiper and life rafts. I could name many more (thanks to a certain search engine) but my point is that I know women have contributed lots.

Back when women had few or no rights lots of female inventions were registered in the name of their husband or father as women were not allowed to own property which included intellectual property, obviously this is wrong and is no longer the case.

So back to women's right;

Should women have the right to vote? – of course they should

Should women have equal pay? – yes, but only if they can actually do the job to the same standard as a man. (Passing an easier test is not equality)

Should women have the same job opportunities as men? – Yes, but again only if they can actually do it.

Intellectually men and women are equal, women seem to do better at formal exams and men seem to do better at practical stuff, but there isn't really much to choose from, so why are most top jobs occupied by men? I personally think there are a few reasons;

More men than women get jobs in business, therefore there is more chance of the most gifted being a man, some women are truly exceptional but if there are more men available then more gifted men will be promoted - basic maths. People will point out that the percentage of women at the top is less than the percentage of women in the workplace, and they are correct but there are more factors to think about.

I am going to get in so much trouble for this but, women are affected by hormonal change, this can and does lead to change in behaviour and judgement, it may not be PC to say and it may not be fair, but it is true.

Women have babies, a baby will stop a women working for a few months and then will take attention for the rest of its life, there are some stay at home fathers but not many. Lots of companies will never employ a lady of child bearing age because it is just too expensive in money, time and efficiency. The maternity laws are ludicrous.

I run a small company and I once looked at taking someone on full time, I looked at the figures for employing someone and decided I could just about afford to employ someone, I am sure that the government would want me to do this, however I would never employ a woman who might have children as the possible maternity bill is too expensive, I would need to take a new person on to cover the job and also pay maternity, where is that extra money supposed to come from? Pregnant employees are also entitled to lots of time off for pregnancy related issues, I agree that maternity and children are very important but financially it does not work for businesses, especially small ones, it isn't about being mean it's about being realistic.

And then we get to sex discrimination, it seems to be one of the biggest growth industries in the U.K.

I work in one of the least P.C. industries there are, the banter between workers is brutal, sexist, regionalist, racist and generally what the P.C brigade would call unacceptable and inappropriate, and yet we are all usually great friends, there is very little offence taken and we function in a high pressure environment to a high degree of professionalism working with people of all races, all religions, men, women, straight, gay and to be honest some downright weird people. Some people would say that I'm one of the weird ones, they may be correct.

The problem with women's rights is that whereas originally it was about equality in conditions, pay and prospects that is no longer the case, it is now mainly about third rate solicitors looking for a way to sue a company for an imagined or even fabricated slight or insult.

To sum up;

If you can do the job then you should be allowed to, if you cannot do the job then no one should be forced to employ you just because you are female, or male, or black, or white or any other reason. Positive discrimination is dumb, counterproductive, causes resentment from the person who actually can do the job but isn't from the correct sex or minority and brings the standard of the whole system down.

Plain dumb.

Is it ok for a man to hit a woman?

Surely in this world of equality it is perfectly acceptable?

Of course it isn't, Just like it isn't ok to hit a man.

But if a woman hits a man and assumes he won't retaliate because she is a woman, is he within his rights to hit her back? I'm afraid he is ladies.

If a woman hits a man then why should he just take it? knock her out mate.

The reason I bring this up is I was thinking about the downsides of equality, there are quite a few:-

The age of retirement has gone from 60 to 65 and is going to rise further, didn't really think this through did you girls?

So;-

Open your own doors

Stand whilst I sit

Carry your own bags

Buy your own drinks

Put the bins out

Paint the house

Dig the garden

Unblock the sink

Fix the car

Build a shed

Catch the spider

Change the lightbulb

All this for a vote that lots of you don't use and the right to be a fire fighter.

But just for the record, I would never hit a woman.

America

The United States Of America.

Land of The Free, the world's policeman,

Give me your tired, your poor, your huddled masses yearning to breathe free, The wretched refuse of your teeming shore. Send these, the homeless, tempest tossed to me, I lift the lamp beside the golden door!

This is the inscription on the Statue of Liberty

It doesn't really ring true does it?

At this moment there are between 11 million and 12 million illegal immigrants in the U.S.A. This is in a country that prides itself on being the place where anyone can make it to the top via the American Dream

At this moment there are between 500,000 and 1 million people homeless in the U.S.A. many of these people have mental health problems and there are massive problems with alcohol abuse and with drug abuse.

At this moment only around 38% of Americans have passports but American influence is felt in almost every corner of the world.

America is a country full of contradictions:-

Land of the free but you have to carry an I.D. card

Guaranteed free speech but music is censored

Another thing that is impossible to miss is the number of seriously obese people that there are, I'm not talking a bit fat or chubby, I'm talking about people who are 3,4 or even 5 times the size they should be, people so fat that they struggle to fit through doorways. I am totally bemused how anyone can allow themselves to get so big, I, like most people have at times noticed my clothes were getting tight and my reaction is to do something about it, I eat better, drink less beer, do a bit of exercise and the weight comes off and all is well. I am far from being a health freak and I am not obsessive about it, I think it is just a normal response. Not once did I think the solution was to buy bigger clothes, but that is what seems to happen a lot in America. I am aware that the UK and other countries have too many obese people but the number in the states is staggering.

The declaration of independence says ''all men are created equal, and have the right to life, liberty and the pursuit of happiness'' But try being an illegal, or black, or Muslim, or Gay or Hispanic. The problem is that when this was written the authors were all white, Christian Straight guys. Black people were considered property with no rights and being Gay was considered to be against the will of God (and still is in some states.)

Now don't get me wrong, America has some great attributes, it just isn't a good place to get ill or have mental health issues or be black in some states or non Christian in others.

This is the country where your rights to be a bigoted racist are protected by the constitution but your rights to be eat a burger in McDonalds without being shot are not.

This is the country where you can legally buy an assault rifle and bullets but not a chocolate egg as the toy inside might be dangerous to children.

This is the country where you need to produce I.D. to buy a beer that tastes like crap but if you want a handgun just go to a gun fair and there will be no background checks at all.

This is also the country that funded the IRA for 30 years casing death and destruction in the UK but declared a war on terror when a few deranged Arabs crashed a couple of planes into the twin towers. I am not willing to call them Muslims for the same reason I don't refer to Hitler as a Christian.

One positive outcome of the twin towers destruction was the almost instant drying up of the IRA funds, I personally believe this to be the main reason for the peace agreement in Northern Ireland.

I am not for one moment condoning terrorism but it didn't seem to matter when it was in other countries.

Now I'm sure this sounds like I am anti American, this could not be further from the truth.

America leads the world in so many fields:-

Computer software and hardware are predominantly American, at least the companies are, most of the hardware seems to be built in the far East. However Apple and Microsoft pretty much are involved to some degree in every product out there, oh and Google, and the internet (though it kind of started in the UK)

Space exploration, other countries are catching up but America is still the world leader and will be for some time.

Medicine is dominated by America as it is massively funded, some would say at the expense of the poorest.

American inventions is a list that could fill a complete book, some of the most interesting to me are;

Barbed wire (there must be millions of miles of it)

Dental floss (for that perfect all American smile)

Credit cards (who doesn't have one?)

Machine guns (I have no words)

Laser printer (can print stuff)

Napalm (possibly the evilest invention ever)

Parking meter (oh thank you)

I could go on for ever but safe to say without American innovation the world would be a lot more laborious.

However it might be a little safer, other American inventions are terms like "friendly fire and collateral damage"

The American armed forces have long had a reputation for shooting anything that moves, in both gulf/Iraq wars more British soldiers were killed by Americans than by Iraqis. Weirdly I put this down to the American press, the American press have overblown the dangers of America to such a degree that they see dangers on every corner. This seems to mean that the prevalent gungho attitude is permeated throughout American society and "shoot first ask questions later" is the norm rather than the exception.

When I have worked in America I have found it to be an interesting experience, almost every person I have met is polite and friendly, I have never seen any evidence of the much publicised racism that is apparently prevalent there. What I have noticed is that almost every American I have met does not identify themselves as an American, We have African Americans, Irish Americans, Italian Americans, Mexican Americans and of course Native Americans. Surely all these different groups are a root cause of racism? When you split people into racial groups then racial attitudes are bound to form. Maybe if everyone just identified themselves as American irrespective of origin then there would be less division?

In the UK we have a perception of the USA that is of the KKK lynching random blacks and race riots and the Police beating up minorities.

Of course we know that is not really how it is but the press never report good things.

I am aware that random events of racism do happen and the "black lives matter" movement is a valid response to that. But in general I have found the

American people to be friendly, welcoming and decent people.

BUT, some things in the USA are downright stupid:-

The education system springs to mind, it doesn't seem to encourage free thinking or innovation. I have met some seriously intelligent people in the states but their knowledge of any subject but their own specialisation is almost zero. I was once asked where I was from and on answering England was asked if I had driven there! The average Americans knowledge of anything outside of America is almost zero.Once again the press is also partly to blame for this.

Guns, The second amendment says "A well regulated Militia,being necessary to the security of a free state, the right to keep and bear arms, shall not be infringed" this does not say you have a right to an AK47 assault rifle, nor does it say that fully automatic handguns and machine pistols are allowed. When this amendment was written the arms in question were flintlock pistols and rifles. Also it is an amendment, which means it can be amended again, just like prohibition. America is the only country in the world which allows unlimited access to weapons, People who are on FBI no fly lists can still buy guns, unbelievable!

Healthcare, American hospitals are some of the best in the world, the doctors and nurses are highly trained and offer a health service second to none, IF you happen to be rich.

We have all heard the old adage of ambulance crews asking for a credit card before they will take you to hospital, I wish I could say it was groundless, but it does happen. If you are unlucky enough to need treatment in the USA you had better be able to pay for it!

This is in the worlds richest country.

And then we get to sports!

Now I am not for one second saying that America is not the world leader in some sports, swimming and athletics spring to mind. But it's the national sports that I don't understand.

American football, it is dreadful, fat blokes with body armour running (slowly) at each other. I can think of no other sport where each side has 2 teams, plus some other special players(kickers etc) it is totally arranged around TV coverage to get as many commercials in as possible. Anybody who has ever watched rugby is bemused by all the padding and helmets, It just makes the whole game slow and boring. I would admit that the guy throwing the ball has some skill but that is about it.

Baseball, it is a girls game called rounders in the rest of the world. I recently went to a baseball game and to be honest i was bored to death, if we hadn't got beer I would have been suicidal.

I am not a fan of cricket but I can appreciate the skill needed to play it, the 2 games are similar in some ways and the scoring of baseball is based on cricket scoring, and they are both boring as hell. I know that the pitcher has skill and hitting a ball moving that speed is also difficult. But catching the ball with a leather bucket strapped to your hand is just pointless, and still they miss! Unbelievable.

Another problem with the U.S.A. is the stranglehold that the unions have in some industries, all the hype we hear about "The American Dream" is made a mockery of by the union networks of nepotism and corruption. I have seen places where all the high paying jobs are taken by one single family. People are given jobs not because they can do them but because they have a familial connection, the level of incompetence this allows is staggering and there is no way to remove these people. It is also the case that seniority is enforced, basically that means if you have been there the longest, you get the top job, even if you are a total imbecile, and they usually are!

Would you bother to get good at a job if you could not be fired?

And then we get to Mr Trump!

Genius ?

Imbecile ?

Entrepreneur ?

Luckiest man ever ?

This man is worth between 500million and 3 billion depending on who you get your figures from, to amass such a fortune you need to be ruthless and astute or luckier than any other person who has ever been born, which is unlikely.

I know he started out with 5 million dollars but even so it takes a certain something to take it to that level.

If Trump had stood against any one other than Mrs Clinton I am sure he would have failed, It was really a perfect storm moment with the total lack of credible Republican AND Democratic opposition.

Donald Trump is the president of the most powerful country in the world !!!

Just let that sink in!

And people are surprised that he is trying to do exactly what he said he would!

And finally, what is America good at?

Doughnuts! Yep thats it!

Technology

Correct me if I am wrong, but isn't the whole point of technology to make things easier, to give us more rest and recreation time, to enable us to do less work for more gain and to generally give us a better quality of life?

Shouldn't it help us connect more with our fellow man and make it easier to have a world community of peoples with little or no strife?

It doesn't seem to be working out like that.

Technology seems to be about how many different ways people can be filmed having sex in as many degrading and deviant ways as possible. It seems to be a way for paedophiles and perverts to swap stories and pictures and even videos of our most innocent being used and abused like toys.

It seems to be a way of making us totally dependent on said technology to have even a remote chance of any friends or even lovers. It seems to be a way for fat old people (like me) to put a ten year old picture on a web site to try to attract the opposite sex, in the vain hope that they won't notice the extra pounds and wrinkles when they eventually meet.

It seems to be a way for companies to bombard us with advertisements for things we neither want nor need just because we once glanced at something similar on Amazon.

It seems to be a way for groups of fraudsters and scammers to get us to help them retrieve countless millions of pounds/dollars from foreign bank accounts in return for a percentage if we would just give them all of our personal details or even a few thousand pounds to help the process.

It seems like there is a massive market for pills to give us a bigger penis or other pills to make it work properly or even other pills to let us use them with people who are not remotely interested in allowing us to.

It seems that you need a thousand pound computer to play patience or scrabble as the old fashioned way of cards or a board is just not modern enough anymore.

It also seems to be a way for terrorists and other human scum to film acts of barbarism and thuggery in the name of yet another peaceful god or religion, so that they can terrorise us from any far flung place on the planet, or even a way for racist bigoted tossers to provoke these same terrorist scum to even more acts of depravity and carnage.

It is used by every political party from mainstream and some of the more dangerous groups from the far left and the far right to try to influence us to their way of thinking.

Do we really need a global network of computers to see cats doing supposedly funny things or a place for people to post pictures of their dinner each night?

Do we need this same network for people to have very public arguments about the most personal subjects so that all their respective friends and family can join in to make it much worse than when it started? Does anyone have any interest in whether or not I can answer 20 questions about 80's music or not?

Now I do use this network myself, I quite often see little gems such as:-

Daughters/fathers etc are wonderful

Repost if you love your daughter/father etc.

Does it mean I don't love my daughter/mother/son/friend/wife/father/brother if I don't repost a pathetic little homily which tells me to repost if I love them?

Does it bollocks! Load of inane drivel!

But this chapter is about technology in general, not just the internet, though I could go on for hours about just that.

I get lost everywhere I go. I have the worst sense of direction on the planet, I can walk into a room and 2 minutes later walk out and go the wrong direction to where I have just been.

 So satnavs are the best invention ever for me. At least they should be, I recently was driving somewhere and my Satnav directed me down a lane which got smaller and smaller until it turned into a path a goat would struggle to get down, I then had to reverse about 2 miles until I found somewhere to turn round. This would never happen with a map, with a map I would stick to real roads and never venture down anything not clearly marked on the map, but I admit it was my fault really for being dumb!

Quite a lot of taxi drivers and coach and truck drivers now use satnavs which is fine some of the time, but no one seems to know how to use a map anymore. I have seen professional drivers stuck at junctions because the satnav has broken and they have no idea where to go. I could be wrong but surely professional drivers should know how to read a map?

Technology also now allows me to ring up British Telecom if I have a problem with my line or broadband, this connects me to someone on the Indian sub continent who barely speaks English, cannot pronounce my name, has no idea where in the country I am and is on such low wages that he has no interest even if I do manage to get him to understand my Lancashire accent. Weirdly enough the guy in a similar place just around the corner from him, who rings me seems to know more about me than my mother and is always helpfully diagnosing problems on my computer which he can fix for free if I give him remote access to my computer.

Though he still can't pronounce my name.

I can now track any deliveries that I am expecting but that doesn't seem to get them to me sooner, though it does mean I can see which wrong depot it has gone to. Knowing my parcel which was posted 50 miles away is now 200 miles away sat in a depot which is closed for bank holidays till next Tuesday does not in any way improve the service I am being provided with.

When I left school no one had a mobile phone, so obviously no one had any of the aps that go with them, because of smart phones (with dumb owners) everything is now done differently. When I went on holiday as a child we used to take pictures, after waiting a week or so we would have those pictures developed and would put them in an album or more frequently a shoebox in the bottom of the wardrobe. Once in a while we would get them out again and look back fondly at our shared experience. Contrast that with today, we take a lot more pictures on our phones, we delete the bad ones and never really look at the good ones ever again, the less computer savvy amongst us then lose them all when we upgrade our phones. Almost no one takes the trouble to actually print any pictures off to look at or even put on a desk or a wall.

I think something has been lost here.

The other problem with mobile phones is that they rule our lives, we are forever checking to see if we have mail, looking to see if anyone has liked our status and checking if anyone has liked us on Tinder/match.com or similar. This obsession has made us anti social, rude and much less aware of our surroundings.

Imagine telling your grandfather that people would be regularly killed in traffic accidents because they were checking text messages on a tiny screen whilst driving, he would think you were mad.

As I'm not the best looking guy in the world I have only had my limited success with the ladies by making them laugh and generally being a cheeky bugger. This is quite hard to do when it's a 2 second look at a picture before swiping right or usually left, I wonder how many perfect couples never meet because they are too busy staring at photos of strangers whilst their perfect soul mate is sitting opposite on the train?

Again I think something has been lost here.

I will never forget the excitement of going to Woolworths or Boots to buy a single from the record department (yes Boots used to sell records)

I would walk into the town centre and spend ages looking through the records on display before eventually buying one. I would then go home and play it for about 2 hours till my dad told me to "turn that bloody rubbish off". Selecting a single was a big deal as I could only afford 1 every couple of weeks. Single sales at this time were regularly between 3 and 5 million for each song in the UK alone. The sound quality on these singles was warmer and somehow more personal than the digital cold sound we now get. These days music has lost its magic, when you can download any song or album for nothing it doesn't have any worth anymore. Downloading music has also turned just about everybody into a thief.

Something has definitely been lost here.

The only advantage for me is that bands tour more as it's the only way they make money. But the budgets are much smaller as they need to make profit from the tour, they used to try to just break even as touring was pretty much a way of promoting their new album or single.

When I was growing up my parents had very little money, therefore my father had a car that was very inexpensive, it would constantly break down but as my father was a keen amateur mechanic he could usually fix it. He would open the bonnet and quickly fix whatever was wrong with it, contrast that to cars today, admittedly they are more reliable but when they do break you open the bonnet, stare at it for a while, scratch your head and then ring someone with a computer who can see what is wrong with it. It takes forever, costs the earth and you have no idea what has been done. I must point out that my father's constant meddling might have caused some of the problems in the first place.

Maybe something has been added here (sorry dad)

A couple of years ago the massive craze in the gaming world was playing guitar hero on the Playstation or X box. I saw loads of people spend hours and hours practising and competing to play a fake guitar, pressing buttons on a guitar shaped controller. All of the people watching would applaud and congratulate the player on their skill and musical prowess. The only problem is that they didn't have any musical prowess, if they had put the same amount of time and energy into actually learning to play the guitar it might have had better results. When I mentioned this I was looked at like I'd suggested we all get naked and play hide the sausage.

Something has gone very wrong here

.

And i'd like to say a little about technology that is totally unneeded and actually makes things worse:-

Automatic soap dispensers, you put your hand under it, nothing happens so you move away, it then drops soap on the counter/floor. You try again and get enough soap to wash the hand of a small mouse. You then go to the automatic tap and get splashed with a teaspoon full of water, you wave hour hand around for what seems like 10 minutes. You then get water flow and wash your hands, as you walk away the tap is still running, you go to the automatic towel dispenser which you wave your hand in front of for a while until it dispenses about 4 inches of paper towel, you pull this and rip it in half, you try again and have the same result, you dry your hands on your trousers and leave the bathroom, the tap is still running.

Electronic Cigarettes / Vapour twigs, Have you ever seen any normal human manage to look so dumb in your life?

So we found out that smoking is really bad for you, quite a long time ago too, so rather than quit smoking they get what looks like a rusty padlock and suck foul smelling steam into our mouths instead. When they breath out they make a cloud big enough to envelop a small car and wonder why normal people object to it. But it is better than smoking I hear you shout! No it isn't, there is now documented evidence of young people starting on E-Cigaretes and moving on to the real thing, I fail to see this as progress.

Not all technology is bad, in spite of how I may seem I read a lot of books, I used to carry 10 or 15 books away on holiday and obviously carrying 1000 books would be impossible but my Kindle allows me to do this, it is my favourite thing. Medical equipment is obviously a good thing and the advancements there are amazing, Self drive cars are coming and apart from everyone losing the ability to drive they might be a good thing, until the hackers start playing with them.

Without technology Stephen Hawking would be another guy in a wheelchair and we would not know him for the undoubted genius that he is.

Without technology science fiction films would be pretty boring affairs, that's if we had films.

Without technology we couldn't see how funny cats can be- hmm

Without technology we couldn't send men into space and ships to Mars, or send back the images and analyse the air and soil.

We are living in a world where technology improves and upgrades at an exponential rate, when you buy a new computer it is obsolete before you get it home, your smartphone is hundreds of times more powerful than the computer you had 10 years ago. Your new car can park itself. Your music is played off your phone to speakers without wires. Your new fridge can order food as you use it. Your vacuum cleaner will operate without your help and can even have a camera so you can look at your house from the pub or on holiday. Your lawn mower will cut the grass at regular intervals, will put itself on charge and never even needs emptying! how the hell does that work?

But I do like my Kindle.

The "Free" Press and Schools

Putting these 2 subjects together might seem a bit odd at first glance, but it isn't as they are our 2 main sources of information and education, or they should be.

But schools don't seem to teach much anymore and newspapers seem intent on dumbing everything down to the lowest possible level.

You are having a laugh!

After spending a considerable amount of time in America and Australia I realise that our press could be a lot worse. But the press in those countries is so bad that it's like being proud of being a better baby sitter than Moira Hindley.

The general lack of general knowledge and current affairs is deplorable in this country.

I have met people who think the Welsh flag is blue.

People who have never heard of an event in 1066.

People who can't tell the time.

People who don't know the colours of the rainbow.

People who don't know the moon goes around the earth,

Or the earth goes around the sun, acceptable in 1066 but not now.

People who cannot tie their shoe laces (Parents I suppose)

People who don't know beef comes from cows, or eggs from chickens.

When I was at school we were continually bombarded with information, this was about world events and maths and history and geography and every other subject you can think of. I am not saying for a second that we remembered it all but even the most challenged of us managed to pick up a smattering of it.

But schools are not about that anymore, schools are about political correctness, passing exams but not necessarily learning much about the subject you are passing. They are about ticking boxes to show you have complied with the latest targets and proving you are diverse and multicultural. They are about making sure little Johnny has not had his feelings hurt or little Lisa has the same chances in life as her male peers. They are almost totally taught by unqualified teaching assistants while the teachers fill in forms and make sure the health and safety information has been filled in just in case little Kevin's mummy sues the school because he stabbed himself with a pencil. They are about providing a safe space where sensitive children can sit without fear of being upset by nasty words. They are about stifling creativity in a "one size fits all" education system that Lenin would be proud of.

They are not about teaching.

People are leaving British schools with no knowledge of the British empire, how is that possible?

The British Empire was the biggest Empire this world has ever seen, or is likely to see. For good or bad that is the truth, so it should be taught. History is not about nice things, it isn't about bad things either.

History is just about truth and should be taught in all its good, evil and interesting glory. If past events are deemed wrong then so be it, but they should still be taught. The British empire did some truly despicable and evil things, but it did some truly amazing things too.

Can you imagine an American child not knowing about The Gettysburg address or George Washington? And it is all down to our old friend Political correctness.

I recently was asked to help with my daughters homework, now when I was at school I was lucky enough to find maths incredibly easy, so I approached her with a degree of confidence.

How Naive I was!

The way Maths is taught now is just madness, It involves about 5 times as much effort as it used to, it takes up pages and pages and is harder to do. It involves columns and lines and lines of figures that we didn't seem to need when I was a child.

No one, and I really do mean No One seems to know why we changed, we are constantly told about the severe lack of maths teachers in our country and maybe, just maybe this is why? Until the current crop of children are old enough to teach there is no one available who can do it in the current method. Though it will probably change again before they are old enough, hopefully back to the old sensible way.

I would like to point out that I am not having a go at the teachers here. I know quite a few teachers personally and I know they work very hard and that they share my frustrations with the political football that is education. However I also work hard as do most people but we don't get a quarter of the year off in paid holidays so I'm not going to defend them too much.

So thats education (or a lack of it)

The Free Press are a bloody joke.

It is ridiculous to use the "catch all" umbrella of the "free" press to justify any of the following:-

Taking pictures of sunbathing celebrities.

Hacking kidnapped children phones.

Character assassination of suspects (yes suspects, not convicted people)

Lying to sell papers.

Lying to further political agendas.

Advertising under the guise of a story.

Promote racial tensions whilst pretending to be condemning them.

If we are to believe the press then they are there to provide a public service to keep us informed of current events in a fair and unbiased way. Any opinions will only be in the opinion column and not in the way the story is written. Does anyone actually believe that?

Every newspaper seems to have an agenda, you can pick up 2 newspapers with an article in each about exactly the same event and they will be 2 totally different stories. If you only read one, as most people do, then what chance do you have of ever reading the truth?

Now we know that some papers are worse than others, but the problem is that the worst culprits are also the best selling. So is the general dumbing down of the country a result of the papers dumbing down, or are the papers dumbing down to meet the demands of a dumb nation?

I am aware that there are some decent, hard working and fair journalists out there, some of the scandals exposed by newspapers have definitely been in the public interest and for this a free press is invaluable.

But lets look at some less relevant items.

Todays daily mail has a full page spread on page 3 about a lamb that sleeps with a dog, with a picture in case you can't visualise it, Page 3!

The daily mirror once held the front page for a picture of Diana's head (the back)

The Sun can still not be bought on Merseyside for reasons we all know.

The News of the world had to be shut down as it crossed lines even the other gutter press wouldn't.

We have articles on sexy female underwear on the same page as calls for women equality.

We have front page news about the Kardashians whilst stories of terrorism and murder are on page 6 - if that page isn't needed for a picture of a funny cat.

It seems to be more important which footballer is Shagging his brothers wife than what the United Nations are doing about Syria.

Newspapers are so full of their own perceived importance that they think they can print and invent whatever they like as the "free" press is untouchable.

When a paper gets it wrong and someone has the temerity to complain there is an outcry, "The free press is a cornerstone of our democracy" is the usual self important cry.

Unfortunately that is true, however it does't mean they should be untouchable.

When a paper incorrectly or unfairly causes embarrassment or financial damage to a person or company they should be punished properly.

Any retractions should be printed on the front page and be twice the size of the original article (I am sure we can print that fluffy cat another day)

They should pay double the cost of any financial losses and they should have to print an apology every day for a week.

And of course we have the obsession the British press has with the royal family. (especially you BBC)

It has just been announced that Prince Philip is to retire from royal duties.

Personally I don't care, but I am aware that some people do.

That does not make it the most important story on the same day that Trump bombs Syria and threatens North Korea.

It is not more important than Education funding (for all the good it does)

Or more pressing than the state of the NHS.

Our head of state is the Queen, he is merely her consort, I wish him my very best as I would any other elderly gentleman but it really isn't news. By all means mention it as the human interest fluff after the real news but not as the lead story surely?

"I wonder what the Kardashians are doing?" is not something I have ever thought, nor do I care which colour of lipstick Posh spice is using, I don't care what any footballers wife is doing nor should I.

And yet the press seem to think I am obsessing over these "facts" like a teenage girl (apologies to teenage girls)

There are certain magazines which specialise in celebrity tittle tattle, I think they are total drivel but if you want to read them then that is fine, but putting this twaddle in a newspaper is totally unacceptable,

So bloody stop it!

The press are responsible for making people famous who have never done anything to justify it.

In an age where everybody can name all the Kardashians hardly anyone knows who discovered Electricity or who first landed on the moon.

We know who Wayne Rooney is married to but not who pioneered test tube babies.

We Know the words to Take That's new song but not who said "we shall fight them on the beaches……."

We know that this years must have accessory is different colour on one fingernail but not what Marie Curie did nor why it killed her.

We can get an A in maths but struggle to add 2 numbers without a calculator.

It was Churchill.

Policing and the courts.

It is a shame that the police are let down so badly by the system.

The police force do a great job but countless different governments have manipulated and abused them to a degree where their job is impossible. They are encouraged to make more arrests and because they are given targets they enforce the laws that target the smallest crimes more stringently as they are easier to get a result. It is much easier to give an on the spot fine for littering than it is to catch a burglar but it looks like an arrest on the crime figures. It is also the case that when the police actually do make a real arrest then the chance of an actual conviction is low as the law is totally in favour of criminals. And if a conviction is achieved then the court usually gives a laughably short sentence which is then cut short by parole assuming it isn't suspended in the first place.

So apparently we are supposed to call them the police service rather than the police force as this is less threatening. Why? They should be threatening, when I was a child we were scared of the police as there was every chance if they caught you doing some minor crime they would give us a slap, and rightly so. If kids are caught now they are treated like guests at a holiday resort and they have absolutely no respect for the law. I am not suggesting that all kids are like that but there is a large minority who are, and we all know how they will turn out as adults. And the governments advice? Give them a hug! I wouldn't recommend it, You are more likely to be pickpockets or stabbed.

When I was growing up there were police officers everywhere, riding bikes, walking the streets and driving around. Where are they all? They are sat in the station filling out forms and crossing t's and ticking boxes. Not that much of a visible deterrent really. But Poundland has a cardboard cutout of a copper in the window so that should be fine then. It is laughable, The lack of visible policing in this country is appalling, It is so bad that the cardboard cutout is so commonplace that we don't even bat an eyelid at it. this is not the fault of the police, it is the fault of interfering busybodies such as the P.C. brigade (no pun intended) It is the fault of politicians who starve the police of funds and produce targets that don't work. It is not the fault of police officers. But it IS the fault of the Police bosses, they are so far removed from the front line that they have no idea what is happening. They have allowed politicians to impose ridiculous targets and have allowed political correctness to become more important than enforcing the law.

Today the main news is that Ian Brady has died, this made me sad.

I am not sad that this evil piece of scum is dead.

I am not sad that he died in pain.

And I am not sad that he died knowing that he was almost universally hated.

I am sad because he should have been killed years ago.

I am sad because we have paid for his treatment and housing for decades and that our so called "decent" criminals didn't manage to kill him either. I know that the liberal wishy washies will say that a civilised country doesn't have the death penalty. And in most cases they are correct.

But not this one!

Child killers should be killed.

Killing a child can never ever have a justifiable reason.

It isn't something that happens by accident like 2 adults fighting.

It isn't something that goes with the territory like drug gangs or other gang wars.

It isn't the same as a woman coming home to catch her husband with her sister (or brother) and sticking a pair of scissors in his neck.

It isn't even the same level of evil as killing for money.

Even the most cold hearted contract killers will not harm children.

Killing a child is such an evil act that death is the only appropriate punishment, and I don't mean like in America where appeals can go on for 30 years, 1 appeal then bang.

I am willing to debate and argue on most subjects as I could be wrong, but not this one, if you don't agree on this one then I don't even want to engage with you, You are Wrong!

The courts don't make any sense.

Well, they don't!

How can a man be convicted of fraud and receive 10 years in prison and yet in the same week another man who beat his girlfriend so badly that her mother didn't recognise her received a 2 year sentence? Because the law isn't about people, the law is about numbers. Money is deemed more important than people.

I recently saw a case where a man was given a suspended sentence because locking him up would have impacted on his wife's quality of life.

According to a crime prevention think tank there were up to 9,000 suspended sentences for criminals who were committing up to their 15th crime, the crimes listed were for burglary, rape, throwing fireworks into crowds and having strangling a cat and having sex with a dog (erm)

The courts routinely send criminals back into society and then wonder why the crime figures are so bad, Idiots!

If you are caught watching television without a TV License you can be fined up to £1000 plus costs, And yet driving whilst drunk can be a fine as little as £150, this seems backward. As far as I am aware an illegally watched TV has never ran over a group of children walking to school.

A large number of people in this country hate the police, I personally reserve that particular emotion for traffic wardens but we'll come back to that. A large part of the hatred comes from traffic police, the traffic police should be a seperate force, we have almost all been given a ticket for driving at 34 miles per hour in a 30mph zone. If it had been outside a school at 3.30 then fair enough, but in an empty town at 4am they really need to leave us alone. The British motorist is the most taxed, bullied and hounded animal in the world. If the government treated horses or bats in the same way there would be an outrage.

The driving laws in this country are ridiculous, the speed limits are continuously changing and always in a downward direction, this is not about safety, this is about making money, A speed camera in London is estimated to cream up to 3 million pounds a year off the lowly motorist, the anti speed lobby will point out that it is their own fault and it makes us safer, if it actually did make us safer then they wouldn't catch anyone, so it doesn't work does it? The camera in question is for a temporary speed limit which motorists say is not clearly signposted, no surprise there then.

Traffic wardens.

Just typing that makes me angry.

What a bunch of spiteful, small minded, jobsworth and petty bastards they are. They have been spotted ticketing ambulances on emergency calls, hearses stopping to start a funeral by picking up the coffin, vans doing deliveries, ice cream vans serving young children and even a man dropping his sick wife at hospital. They will listen to no mitigating reasons, they don't care if your car is broken, they are not moved by other peoples misery but seem to actually enjoy causing it. Has anybody in the world said to his careers advisor "I want to be a traffic warden" ? I doubt it, You would be thrown out and rightly so.

But apparently there is an even nastier phenomenon in this modern world, They are called PCSO's. They wear the uniform of a P.C. with slight differences, they can issue parking fines, they can arrest someone and in some cases can even use force to enter a premises. BUT……

They don't get paid!

Why would anybody do those things for nothing? Why?

I have no idea, is it to save the country money? Unlikely.

Is it to make the streets a safer place? Doubt it.

Would it be to feel the bond and camaraderie of being in a big boys club? Maybe.

But more likely it is because they want to wear a uniform as it might help get the girls/boys.

And because they like imposing rules and regulations on the public and NCP wouldn't employ them.

But in reality it is the government getting a police presence on the street and paying little for it. But it's dangerous, they are under trained and have no real powers and the real police tend to resent them. Apparently the real police coined the term "lost shoppers" to describe them.

So to the real police;

The vast majority of people are glad you are here

You do an impossible job under very difficult conditions

The vast majority of you are decent and honest but the small minority of bribe taking, suspect beating, racist drug dealers give you all a disproportionate bad name.

However you do get some of the best pension deals in the country and you only need to do 20 years to qualify.

I used to work at a theatre in Manchester, we once had a broken fire door and I was kicking it to get it to close so we could open the main doors to let the audience in. A passing PC grabbed me and said "oh it's you! I thought it was one of those Darkies!" That was my first ever personal experience of what was later called "institutionalised racism" I was genuinely shocked.

Has it changed? I have no idea.

By the way- If when you get married and one of the bridesmaids is a serving police officer, tell your best man before he does his speech about your past adventures, just saying.

Benefits and Beggars

My first wage was £26.25 per week, this was in 1984. Out of that vast amount I paid £10 to my parents for food, electricity, rent, cleaning, lifts to and fro, clothes washing and everything else decent parents do for their children. I'm pretty sure my parents should have received more but it was just a token really to help me realise that you get nothing for free. So I was left with £16.25 per week to buy clothes, entertainment, bus fares (for leisure, work ones were paid by the YTS) and all the other things 16 year olds need to survive. Not a lot of money I'm sure you would agree. And yet I managed, and I managed because my parents had taught me that if you have £10 pounds in your pocket, you cannot spend £11, seems pretty basic doesn't it? Though the Labour party hasn't worked it out yet.

So with that self righteous start to the chapter out of the way, let's have a look at benefits.

I have no problem with looking after and feeding the disabled, the genuine sick and the genuine unemployed. I am quite happy to contribute some of my hard earned cash to give a seriously disabled person a better quality of life. I am more than happy to give money that I earn to feed and house a genuinely sick person and to help raise kids who have no family to help them. I am also willing to feed and house the genuinely unemployed. I am very willing to contribute towards a free to patient NHS for the sick, infirm and the elderly. I am pretty sure I'm going to need it one day, and I shall use it with pride that I helped to pay for it. I am also very happy to pay for and grant asylum to genuine cases where to go back to their country of birth is a death sentence. I am sure you have noticed the word genuine cropping up once or twice; we shall come back to that.

Now having said all of this I am not willing to pay for someone else to drink beer, I might buy the odd round in the pub, but that should be my choice. I am definitely not willing to pay for someone else to smoke, nor am I willing to pay for someone else to watch TV all day or to have a Satellite dish so they can watch pay per view football whilst I'm at work paying for it. I am also not prepared to fund the NHS so that the non workers can clog up the system with drinking and smoking related disease that I have paid for them to get. I am also not prepared to pay for health tourists to visit from overseas to have a baby, receive treatment or even receive palliative care. I really don't think it's my job to pay for foreign people to claim benefits in this country just because it's a nicer place to live. The reason it is a nicer place to live is because the British people have made it so. It wasn't always like this!

But this chapter is really about our home grown scroungers. Why do we have so many? And the answer is quite complicated;

Maybe because you can receive more money sitting on your arse than you can earn on minimum wage. Or because some parents don't teach their children a sense of pride, I know people who would rather work for £100 per week than receive £500 per week in benefits. But they are a rare case. Or because child support encourages people to have children. Or maybe because anyone who does try to make a living is penalised with high taxes, and then sees those taxes wasted on lazy people and stupid government schemes.

So what is the solution?

Firstly the minimum wage should be higher for a 40 hour week than anyone can receive on benefits. And that should be achieved by raising the minimum wage a little and cutting benefits a lot.

The minimum wage should enable a man or woman to feed, clothe and house them with a little left over.

What about the children though? That's easy; if you can't afford to feed a child then don't have one. It is not a God given right to be a parent. If you cannot afford a child then it is NOT my place to pay for one for you. Whilst we are on the subject it is not a God given right to own a dog either, last time I checked pet food was expensive, if you cannot afford a dog then don't get one.

Tax credits should not exist, by all means raise the threshold when people pay tax and have a lower rate, tax credits are just another layer of bureaucracy that we don't need.

I sometimes pick my son up from school, to do this I have to drive through one of the largest council estates in Europe, you can easily see which houses are rented by hard working decent people, the gardens are tidy, the car in front is well kept and everything is clean and orderly, and the 1 or 2 children who come out of these houses to join my son at school are well presented, polite and well behaved.

You can also tell which houses are provided free of charge by the council, the gardens are a mess, and in the summer will have a group of people in them smoking and drinking lager and playing music loudly. There is a satellite dish on the front of the house. The cars, yes always more than 1 are souped up Subaru's or Astra's with 12 spotlights. The house will look dirty and the 5 or 6 children will be wearing baseball caps and track suits. These children will be rude and scruffy and be disruptive at school.

Ok I might be stereotyping a little bit, but not much. I know that there are rare cases where an exceptional student comes from a disadvantaged background. By the way I grew up on a council estate and my parents still live on one, I know there are many decent, civil, polite hard working people living there, my parents are the hardest working people I've ever met and it disgusts me that they are entitled to less than some of their neighbours who have never done a day's work in their lives, just because they had the brains to save a little for their retirement.

The problem is that benefits are too generous and paid in cash.

As a claimant you should receive a place to live, it should be a small house with no garden, I know many people who work hard and cannot afford a house with a garden. Rather than cash you should receive food stamps with your name on them which can only be exchanged for food and household goods. These could only be spent by you on proof of ID. This should be calculated to provide for the number of people in your household. You should not be able to purchase alcohol or cigarettes with these stamps. Any more than that should be worked for; the council always has need of labor, so they should provide small part time jobs at minimum wage for a few hours per week, paid in cash, if you want money for beer and cigarettes then work for it.

When I was 20 I could afford to go out once a week or twice if I was lucky, and I was working, I see people in the local pubs almost every night and I know they have never had a job.

That is just wrong!

I never give money to beggars, I sometimes give money to Big Issue sellers, and I usually give money to buskers, because buskers are doing something to earn the money. Beggars are just scrounging, and there is no excuse for that. I have also noticed that a large number of beggars have a dog with them, if you cannot feed yourself then how can you feed a dog? And isn't it strange how beggars are always sitting next to a cash machine?

Now there are some homeless people out there with mental health issues and those people being on the streets is a national disgrace, these people desperately need help and I am more than happy to contribute to help fund it. However, anyone who is sleeping rough because they are drug addicts and alcoholics do not deserve my help. I like to have a beer, I have been known to drink too much and have made myself ill on a number of occasions by drinking more than I should. Not once have I thought that is anybody's fault but my own. In spite of being surrounded by drugs since I was about 16 I have never been retarded enough to try them, but if I had I wouldn't expect anyone else to pay for me. Once again this is about people having responsibility for their own actions; if you want to drink till you lose your job or take drugs till you are homeless then that is YOUR choice. I am not willing to pay for you and I cannot believe anyone thinks I should.

People tell me that alcoholism and drug dependency are diseases and that we should treat them rather than penalise them. Correct me if I am wrong but everybody knows that heroin is highly addictive and that drinking too much can lead to alcoholism? The first time you use heroin that is a choice, it is a choice where you know that it could lead to addiction and all the associated problems, Heroin is also illegal and therefore you are also a criminal and should be treated as such. Alcoholism is slightly different as it is legal and lots of people can drink to excess without getting addicted. But it is still your choice to drink or not.

I know there is a small minority of people sleeping on the streets who are there through no fault of their own, people do fall through the cracks. There does not seem to be enough resources to help these genuine cases but that is because so much is wasted on the lazy and scrounging majority. We need to prioritise better.

Then we get to my favourite topic, people who are too fat to work.

I have absolutely no interest in feeding, housing or looking after someone who is such a lazy, fat slob that they cannot work, Obesity is not a disease, eating burgers and pizzas every day and drinking gallons of cola and beer is just gluttony.

Any parent with a fat child should be prosecuted for cruelty and the children should be taken away. I am not talking about children who are a bit chubby, we have all seen a family of seriously fat people walking (or being wheeled) around town, the fat dad who still has a bit of muscle left and the mum who looks like a circus tent on short fat legs, followed by the 2 or 3 children who are like baby elephants. Having seriously fat children is child abuse, it has long term health consequences and also ruins the quality of life for yet another generation.

Assuming anyone ever reads this, and I'm not overly confident, then I can see a herd of wildebeest like proportions getting angry and offended by this, but unless I'm encircled I fancy my chances of escaping, but if I inspire just one fatty to get fit so they can catch me then i'll be happy.

So as I threatened we come back to the word Genuine.

There have been countless cases of people on disability allowance being caught dancing, skiing, driving taxis and forklifts, body building and even parachuting. Is it just me who is flabbergasted by this?

It seems that anyone can just go to the doctors and say they have a bad back and get signed off work indefinitely, this is such a prevalent problem that it is reported almost daily. When these people are caught they should be charged with theft and should be made to work the full amount off, with interest and then get sent to prison where they should also charged for the cost of their imprisonment.

If they can't pay then they should be made to pay it back at a reasonable rate, not 5 pence a month as the courts allow with fines. If we don't have severe punishments then there is no deterrent.

There are some people who have absolutely no intention of ever ever doing a days work, these people will do anything to avoid working, they pretend to look for jobs, they pretend to be ill or injured, they deliberately fail interviews when they are made to go for them and on the rare occasion they get a job they get sacked as quick as possible. I wonder what would happen if we didn't give them money? Not a bloody penny. These people exist because no matter how lazy, selfish and self centred they are, they know we will still feed them, house them, warm them, provide clothes and even give them money for a television, food and even beer! And if they have kids we will pay them even more, honestly it's true!

These people are the only people who truly deserve to be homeless and starving;

I am not talking about someone who is looking for work and wants nothing more than a fair wage for a days work.

Nor do I mean someone who is out of work because of redundancies or jobs moving abroad (another failure of government)

Nor do I mean the uneducated failed by our schools or the injured or genuinely ill.

I mean the people we all know, in the pub all the time, smoking, driving a car, never ever done any work but knows how to play the system. If anyone remembers the T.V. program "Bread" then they know just what I mean. These are also the first people to bleat on about their "rights" Sorry but if you don't contribute when you could then you have none. And I do mean none, I would deny you health care, housing, food, clothes and everything else.

I teach my children to not use the term "hate" as it is a very strong word which shouldn't be used when you mean, slightly annoying or a bit rude, but I truly hate these people.

Worthless scum.

L.G.B.T………

For anyone that doesn't know, that means:

Lesbian, Gay, Bisexual and Transgender.

You would think that would cover just about anyone wouldn't you?

Apparently not, in fact this term is out of date.

We are now supposed to use the term LGBTTQQIAAP.

this stands for:-

Lesbian

Gay

Bisexual

Transgender

Transsexual

Queer

Questioning

Intersex

Asexual

Allies

and Pansexual

what a load of bollocks! (or not as the case may be)

for the confused (in a literary sense not a sexual sense) i will try to explain

We all know that a lesbian who is a female who is attracted to females.

Gay describes a man who is attracted to men.

Bisexuals are attracted to both men and women.

Transgenders are men who feel like women and women who feel like men.

Transexuals are people who have been surgically altered to change sex.

Queer is a derogatory term for homosexuals

Questioning is for people who are not sure what they fancy

Intersex is what we used to refer to as hermaphrodite

Asexual is someone who isn't interested in sex at all

Allies are straight people who support this diverse community

And Pansexuals fancy all the above.

Whew

Now I have no problem with who you fancy, who you sleep with or what you get up to, as long as it is legal, doesn't involve children or animals, and there is consent then I don't think it is my business or anyone else's.

It is definitely not for the government or religious groups to tell us who we should go to bed with. If my next door neighbour wants to have sex with another man/woman/man dressed as a woman or a woman seeing if she likes men or anyone else I really don't think it has any bearing on my life and is therefore nothing to do with me.

But when it does affect my life then I think I'm allowed an opinion, first of all having all these different terms is ridiculous.

There are just 2 sexes!

That's right, 2 not 11 !

A lesbian is still a woman, the fact that she fancies women does't alter that,

The same goes for gay men.

Bisexuals are men or women, they can't be both, just like if I fancied a horse it wouldn't mean you could enter me in the Cheltenham gold cup.

If you choose to wear a dress and makeup or dungarees and a flat cap it does not alter the fact that you are male and female respectively, nor does it matter.

If you have gender reassignment then you may look like the opposite sex to what you were born, you are free to act, dress and identify as your new gender but until a woman can produce sperm and a man can give birth it will not actually be the case. I am not being cruel or insensitive and I would never want to offend just for the sake of it but science is science.

I don't understand why they include Queer in the list as its viewed as a derogatory term.

Questioning, who isn't? Again No idea why this is even included.

Intersex is a birth defect, calling it another sex is like saying that co joined children are a new species.

Allies? thats just people who buy into this rubbish , so basically the sexual P.C.brigade

And Pansexuals, will sleep with anyone, irrespective of gender, gender bias or dress sense, just greedy bastards basically, sexual gluttons.

As I write this there is a furore in the press about which toilets some people should use, there used to be Gents and Ladies but apparently we should have none gender specific toilets available.

No we shouldn't!

For all its faults we live in a democracy, this means if most people want something to happen then it should. We should not bend over backwards to accommodate everyone who is a bit different, whether it is insisting all buildings are designed for disabled access irrespective of whether there will ever be a need for it or building extra toilets for the 0.01% of us who are not sure, or making Vegetarian food available everywhere.

If people want or need special facilities then I have no problem providing them if it is a real need, it is not for society to provide them everywhere on the off chance they might be needed one day.

Disabled access toilets in a climbing centre at the top of a mountain is a prime example, it isn't going to come up, but I've seen them.

So if you need to go to the toilet, just go where you feel comfortable, no one cares. But I do understand the problems, If I was to see a 6 FT burly guy dressed as a woman going into the ladies toilets then I might be a bit worried for the safety of ladies in there, I'm not suggesting that they would be more at risk than from anyone else but it does seem an easy way to abuse the system. I don't know what a happy medium should be, maybe the disabled toilet should be for all people as they are sometimes signed for both men and women anyway.

All these different terms are designed to make people feel more comfortable describing themselves, but what they actually achieve is division and derision. By making such a big deal of it they just highlight differences rather than achieve the inclusion that they are looking for.

GAY PRIDE! Oh grow up!

STRAIGHT PRIDE! it would be just as silly

Again highlighting differences, its like the Black police association, how can a club that only accepts black members promote racial equality, it's ludicrous.

If I got a few hundred people together and we marched through the gay village proclaiming how proud we were to be straight we would be accused of being homophobic.

If a white policeman started a whites only police club he would be accused of racism.

Double standards always cause prejudice.

I understand that being homosexual and being black has not always been easy, I understand that back in the past we needed groups to fight for equal rights for women, blacks, queers, orientals and basically anyone not male, white and Christian. But these organisations are not about equal rights anymore, they are about special rights and that is wrong.

I would like to point out that I have many friends who are gay, I have attended lesbian weddings, I have spent many an enjoyable evening in the gay village in Manchester.

I do not care what sex you are, or who you want to sleep with, I am not interested if you feel like you are male, female, neither, both or something else, but don't ask for special treatment or special rights, that isn't equality.

And then there are the fashionably gay.

A hundred years ago people of anything other than straight persuasion would hide this from society, they would meet like minded people in secret to avoid persecution and prosecution and obviously that is something society should be ashamed of. But it has now gone the other way, people who are straight pretending to be gay so they can be accepted into that community, it is just as ridiculous.

According to the office for national statistics about 1.5% of people in the U.K are either gay or bisexual. Some other sources put it as high as 6%. But the gay lobby hold a massively disproportionate amount of power. The problem is fear. Anybody who holds anti gay sentiment is too afraid to mention it for fear of the gay lobby, this isn't good for anyone, if someone feels that they find gay sex to be distasteful or against their religious beliefs then they should be allowed to say so. It doesn't matter if I agree with them(I don't) but they should be allowed to speak, it is only by discussion that things change. Gagging free speech on any subject gives peoples skewed views an underground voice which is much harder to fight. If your point of view is correct then it should be able to survive argument and scrutiny, which puts this book at major risk i'm sure.

I grew up in a typical Northern working class town, this did not prepare me for meeting people of different sexual persuasions. Anyone not straight and manly was open to ridicule and even abuse. Obviously we have moved on from there, at least some of us have. Working with people of different sexualities made me realise that the person was much more important than who he or she fancied. An openly gay man once accused me of being homophobic, this was because I was taking the mickey a bit, I pointed out that as I was taking the mickey out of everyone else and If I was to miss him out then that would be a slight in itself. I genuinely do not understand why men are gay, I have no problem with it but I don't understand it, I explained to the man in question that I viewed gay men in the same way I view trainspotters, I will never understand why a man would sit in a train station all day writing down which trains he has seen. In the same way I will never understand why a man would push Holly Willoughby out of the way to get to me. But that doesn't mean I have a problem with it, in fact it increases my chances with her.

All the way up to no chance.

Royalty

King, Prince, Duke, Archduke, Emperor, Queen, Princess, Count, Empress, Earl, Viscount, Baron, Tsar, Caesar and Kaiser.

Where did they come from?

It would appear that back in the day whoever was the leader of the biggest army got to be the boss. Back in the mists of time, I am sure it made sense for this to be an acceptable way to choose who the boss was. Of course the area these bosses ruled was subject to change when a bigger army or better leader appeared. At this time the King would lead his soldiers into battle and would therefore have the right to rule, assuming he won. Lots of Kings were killed, maimed, imprisoned, tortured, executed and crippled. So the risks were equal to the rewards.

Cutting a ribbon to open a new sewage plant isn't quite the same is it?

Now before the royalists have me imprisoned in the tower and executed for treason let me say this, I think the Queen does an admirable job. She appears to be a nice lady and she is respected all over the world to a level that politicians can only dream of. To my Knowledge she has never said anything controversial or done anything that makes the UK look bad in any way, not so sure about her husband but that's another story.

I agree that an elected President would be a worse system; just the thought of President Blair is enough of a reason to keep the monarchy for eternity. Or President Cameron or Milliband for that matter.

But to represent Britain on a global stage does she really need a portfolio of property worth more than 8 billion pounds? Do the British people need to pay for her extended family to occupy grand palaces and estates all over the country? Does the Heir to the throne need to have the Duchy of Cornwall to do what is basically sitting on his royal arse waiting for his mother to abdicate or die? (And I wish her a long happy life)

The Duchy of Cornwall is worth roughly 750 million pounds with an annual profit of around 20 million pounds. That is a very expensive waiting room. The Royalists are going to point out that Prince Charles voluntarily pays income tax even though he is exempt by law. So what? Why should you and I have to pay income tax on our hard work? I personally have worked very hard to get to a stage where I make reasonable money; I started with nothing and have taken huge financial risks to now own a successful company. I was not handed a multi million pound business on a plate.

And this is my problem with Royalty, it isn't fair! No one should be tax exempt, no one should be handed massive estates because they might one day be King.

I can just about cope with having the Queen as I can't think of a better way of doing it, but all of her extended family just seem to me to be a drain on OUR taxes.

People will point out that we have a long tradition of Royal princes serving in the armed forces and that they serve the country in this way, it's funny how they are all naturally gifted and rise through the ranks quicker than the regular working class lads. Prince Charles served in the Navy for 5 years, at the end he was the commanding officer of HMS Bronington. From trainee to Captain in 5 years, that's amazing, he must be exceptionally gifted. But of course he probably isn't, it is just privilege from an accident of birth.

I would like to point out that I have nothing personally against any individual member of the Royal family, however I object to the full system. Military rank should be based on talent, not on what your surname happens to be. That of course is assuming anyone really knows what their last name is; the Queen was born Elizabeth Alexandra Mary Windsor, However her father's last was Wettin, from Saxe-Coburg and Gotha of Germany. Her children use the various surnames of Mountbatten-Windsor, Wessex, Wales or they use their titles instead.

Confusing, the only other people I know who use so many different names are doing it to dodge tax but as we have seen that can't be the case here.

And then there is the Duke of Edinburgh, an impoverished Greek prince who married our queen who is also her distant cousin. Incidentally his real surname is Schleswig-Holstein-Sonderburg-Glucksburg. This man is worth his weight in gold just for some of the racist and bigoted statements he has made over the years; from asking Diversity if they are all one family, asking a trekker in New Guinea if he had managed to not get eaten, to asking a Scottish driving instructor how he kept the natives sober long enough to pass the test.

And his son talks to trees, no wonder.

The Queen does not own a passport; apparently because all passports are issued in her name she doesn't need one. She also does not need a driving licence; that must be because being a queen makes you instantly able to drive.

During the second world war the queen trained as a mechanic and drove trucks to help with the war effort, for that I salute her.

As I am writing this we have just had a state funeral for Richard the 3rd; his body was discovered under a car park. This man was a vicious child murdering throne usurper. But because he was Royal he apparently deserved a lavish and expensive funeral. Richard 3rd was also the last English King to be killed in battle and therefore the last king to actually deserve the title.

I thought it was sad when princess Diana was killed in a car crash in France, I would find it sad if any young mother was killed in those or any other circumstance. Every day mothers from all walks of life die in tragic and horrible ways. Do the children of these normal people suffer any less? I would say they suffer more, most people have money worries that are made much worse by a death in the family, and most people do not have infinite resources to help them cope with an already difficult situation. The amount of press this event received was unbelievable, wars, terrorist acts, famine and genocide all took a second seat in the press for weeks after her death, why is one privileged person's death worth more than thousands of other peoples from all over the world?

The press displayed an unbelievable amount of hypocrisy in this period, before Diana's untimely death the press in general were almost daily printing stories and articles designed to vilify and undermine her at every turn. She was portrayed as a self publicist, a bad mother, an adulterer and much more, most of which turned out to be true but the massive U turn after her death was just opportunism on a grand scale, the collective press should hang their collective head in shame.

We have just had another Royal birth. Whereas I am quite happy to quite happy to congratulate any family on a new arrival I am not so keen when I will be one of the ones paying for her massively privileged upbringing, just as I don't want to pay for scroungers at the other end of the scale to have children either.

However I do wish baby Charlotte a long and happy life, maybe her parents can send me a couple of million pounds to help pay for my children?

I am aware that nobody chooses to be born into the royal family, my issue isn't with the people themselves, my problem is with the whole medieval system.

There are 26 Monarchs in the world whom preside over 43 countries. There is a mixture of constitutional monarchs like are own and outright dictatorships like Tonga and Saudi Arabia, there are also a few where the lines are a little more blurred. I have just found out that officially the Pope is the constitutional monarch of the Vatican which I not only find surprising but also a bit weird.

If we are going to have a monarch and I'm not sure we should, then the one we have is pretty good.

Our Queen does not imprison political dissidents and couldn't even if she wanted to.

She does not have people executed for opposing her (I hope)

She cannot rob the people to further her own bank balance, not that she needs to.

She doesn't subjugate half of the population by forbidding them to drive based on their sex.

She doesn't stop people voting in elections.

She cannot decide to take us to war.

She has never once done or said anything to embarrass us as a country, take note Mr Trump.

So I suppose that even though I hate the whole idea of a monarchy and find the whole institution quite farcical and out dated, even though I get quite annoyed at the massive amount of money that goes to support and prolong the whole thing, even though I don't believe anyone should be handed a career because of an accident of birth, and even though the queen wears some quite frankly weird outfits, I can't think of a better system.

However there are other problems, the British monarchy perpetuates the class system, if we didn't have kings and queens then all the other titles would become obsolete.

We have lots of Dukes, Marquesses, Marchionesses, Earls, Countesses, Viscounts, Viscountesses, Barons, Baronesses and Lords.

We are unrealistically and unreasonably impressed in this country by a title. It doesn't matter if the person in question is a waste of skin or a murderer or thief.

Lord Lucan still causes endless debate and discussion as if he is the first person to ever go missing.

When a Duke or a Earl does something it receives more attention that when a commoner does exactly the same thing, it's bad enough our obsession with celebrity but giving someone attention because they have a made up title is ridiculous.

Another problem is that the Queen is the head of state and also head of the anglican church, how is that not a conflict of interest? The majority of people in the U.K are not members of the Church of England. This means that our head of state is the head of a church with tremendous influence over Anglican people from lots of different countries, She is also the head of the Commonwealth as well as being head of state for some of those countries too which must be confusing as well as yet another conflict of interest.

She is lovely though.

The End Bit

Well that was fun.

I started writing this book as a bit of a laugh really, just having a rant about whatever took my fancy or whatever had annoyed me on that day.

It is sometimes what I really mean, sometimes what I think is a bit funny and sometimes just argumentative for the sake of it.

I hope it makes you think.

I hope it annoys you a bit.

I hope it makes people talk assuming anyone ever reads it.

I don't actually care if just a few of my mates read it so they can give me grief about it.

I am sure it is full of spelling mistakes, bad grammar, mis quotes and spurious facts and figures, but in this world of fake news it is nice to feel included.

This is not meant to be taken too seriously though it does look at some pretty serious subjects. We should do anything we can to combat racism, sexism, anti religious group propaganda, homophobia and all other forms of hate. But it should be done with humour, no one should be exempt from ridicule and satire, positive discrimination is exactly that, discrimination. Just because someone belongs to a majority group is no reason to exclude them as they might still be the best person to fill a position, in fact just by the laws of chance they probably will be.

So chill out.

Have a beer.

Eat a cake.

Be yourself.

Enjoy yourself.

This isn't a practise.

Believe what is right for you, but don't expect everyone to agree,

And don't be bothered when they don't.

Love who you want to love.

Sleep with who you want to (if they want to)

Don't take it too serious.

Don't take others too serious.

Definitely don't take me serious.

So what have I learn't from all this?

I like ranting.

Most people are decent and hard working.

People need to stop being so bloody precious about stuff.

Complaining about being offended over the tiniest thing will make the whole situation worse.

Laughing at yourself is very liberating.

Laughing at others is more fun.

Equality is great when it is real rather than used as an excuse for special treatment.

I need a new hobby, or I might just write another one.

What have you learnt from this?

I'm probably an idiot.

19713932R00132

Printed in Poland
by Amazon Fulfillment
Poland Sp. z o.o., Wrocław